Praise for *Behind the Closed Door*

"Therapists learn a lot about their clients' mental spaces, but rarely address their clients' physical spaces. This systemic professional oversight is truly unfortunate because client well-being is so often dependent not only on what's going on in clients' minds, but also on how their homes, offices, and other living spaces are organized.

In this ground-breaking book, Katie Tracy encourages therapists to get more curious about their clients' desks, closets, and kitchen counters—the material infrastructure that shapes clients' daily lives. Moreover, Ms. Tracy shows therapists how they can make a material difference in these messy-life worlds. This book is based on both academic research and real-world experience. A must-read for the contemporary helping professional."

—AHIR GOPALDAS, PhD, Associate Professor of Marketing,
Gabelli School of Business, Fordham University

"Katie Tracy has an insightful winner in this simple and easy-to-read book. Ms. Tracy sets the stage for mental health professionals to understand how physical space filled with clutter can influence the client's emotional experiences. There are connections between clutter and the client's ability to cope, and this book gives us a straightforward appreciation of that link. Counselors and professional organizers will find this book a resource and tool to help their clients reach their life goals to declutter."

—DR. JOSEPH R FERRARI, Vincent dePaul professor of psychology, DePaul University,
Author of *Still Procrastinating? The No Regrets Guide for Getting It Done*

"This highly readable book reveals the many ways that therapists and professional organizers can work together to not only benefit their mutual clients, but also to enjoy their work more. Katie Tracy insightfully explains how our thoughts and feelings get wrapped up in, hidden by, and twisted together with our belongings and why working on your physical stuff can be inseparable from working on your mental stuff. Whether you are a therapist, professional organizer, or client, this book will bring it all together."

—ARI TUCKMAN, PsyD, CST, Psychologist, ADHD Expert,
Author, and International Speaker

"In *Behind the Closed Door*, professional organizer Katie Tracy weaves together scientific research and her rich experience working with clients to illuminate the cyclical relationship between our emotions and the stuff that clutters our physical spaces. This book reveals the meaningful role organizers can play alongside mental health care professionals to improve individuals' physical and mental well-being."

—CATHERINE ROSTER, Ph.D.
Professor, University of New Mexico

"As a professional organizer and clinical therapist, I both applaud and thank Katie Tracy for focusing in depth on the individual's relationship with their stuff, remaining dedicated to work through this relationship with them, then allowing and supporting them to let go—all the while helping them to understand that they are *so much more than* their stuff. This book serves as an important manual for both the PO *and* the MH professional, as these roles in the client's life are not mutually exclusive. Most POs are not professionally equipped to effectively guide individuals through extreme emotional disregulation that results from their clutter. Most, if not all, MH professionals are not able to fully understand the nature of a client's disorganized chaos because they are not physically in the home to observe the strained client-stuff relationship. With this book, Katie is able to beautifully bridge this gap and provide a comprehensive picture and plan to help clients move forward.

I strongly encourage anyone who struggles themselves with clutter or helps others who do, to take full advantage of her expertise. This is MUST read if you're ready to help a client, or yourself, make some major life changes!"

—RACHEL SAGER, LCSW, Professional Organizer,
RESTART with Rachel

Behind the Closed Door

Behind the Closed Door

The Mental Stress of Physical Stuff

KATIE TRACY, CPO®

Stonebrook Publishing
Saint Louis, Missouri

STONEBROOK
PUBLISHING

A STONEBROOK PUBLISHING BOOK
©2020 Katie Tracy

Library of Congress Control Number: 2020910265
ISBN: 978-1-7322767-9-6

www.stonebrookpublishing.net
PRINTED IN THE UNITED STATES OF AMERICA
10 9 8 7 6 5 4 3 2 1

Dedication

To "Danielle"

Contents

Introduction

THE TITLE OF THIS BOOK, *Behind the Closed Door*, is intentional. Behind the closed door of a therapist's office, clients share intimate parts of their lives: feelings, relationships, insecurities, doubts, and struggles. This mental clutter and the associated stress are common experiences today. Mental health professionals work with clients to wade through their emotions and experiences so they can find clarity and calm inside their minds and lives.

Behind the closed doors of their homes, these clients also hide the physical clutter of their lives: overstuffed closets, basements and garages used for storage, and cluttered living spaces. These closed doors hide the clutter, but also create a barrier to personal satisfaction, better relationships, and overall well-being. The work of professional organizers is to help clients remove the physical barriers of clutter so they can find peace and ease in their homes.

This book shows how two professional worlds—mental health and organizing—go hand in hand, the ways each influences the other, and how each can be a tool to create change in clients' lives. Through collaboration, professionals in both fields can guide their clients to create a mental and physical space that, when the door is closed, the client feels at peace there.

PART 1

Overlapping Worlds

*"A cluttered house might stand as evidence
for (or result in) a disordered mind, and
conversely, that a disordered mind may
lead to a cluttered house."*[1]
— KATIE KILROY-MARAC

CHAPTER 1

The Client Who Changed Everything

I DIDN'T REALIZE AT THE TIME that Danielle would change the entire course of my business and career. Our work started the same as any other client. Danielle was serious about making some big changes in her home life. Fed up with the clutter that she waded through every day, she was ready to make the commitment to change how her home looked and functioned. Her clear goals included making room for then-boyfriend, now husband, Hank, to move in with her. Danielle knew she needed help and interviewed several professional organizers to find one who was a good fit for her.

Danielle was anxious as we met for our assessment appointment. I sensed her heart beating as rapidly as the words and breath that tumbled from her mouth. I started with my usual opening question, "What made you call an organizer? Why do you want to start now?"

"I can't do this on my own. I mean this is all just so. . ." She trailed off as she looked around her apartment. Most rooms in her modest, one-bedroom apartment were cluttered. "It's not that I'm not trying," her voice pleaded. "I throw stuff out. I try to clean up. It just never lasts, and then I get mad at myself. I don't know why I can't do this on my own." She shook her head at herself. "I live here and I don't even like being here."

My business, Simple Spaces, works mostly with women who are very similar to Danielle. They feel frustrated and overwhelmed with their homes due to disorganization and clutter. As a professional organizer I help them purge, sort, reorganize, and systematize. The goal is to help them figure out what to do with all the "stuff" that clutters their homes and, in effect, change their lives.

As we toured her apartment, I felt Danielle's frustration. "I usually don't get home from work until after nine o'clock," she said with weariness in her voice as we walked by the front door. "As soon as I walk in, I drop my stuff here." The small entryway was littered with delivery boxes, shoes, bags, and mail. The bedroom had similar challenges. "I do the wash, but don't get the laundry put away right away, so I end up picking through the basket for clothes to wear. The closet's a mess, so it's just easier to pick from here anyway."

Danielle's dining room was the most interesting. It had typical dining room furniture: a wood table, a small buffet, and a glass front china cabinet, but there were moving boxes everywhere. "When did you move in?" I asked Danielle.

"About four years ago," she said, embarrassed. "I never unpacked these boxes."

"What's in them?" I asked.

She sighed before she answered, "These are from my house before the divorce."

Danielle, in her early forties, was married ten years earlier. It was a whirlwind of a fancy wedding, a big house, and all the things she thought she was supposed to do and have. Within two years the marriage was over.

These boxes were part of the reason she called me: boxed up memories from a broken marriage. She avoided those boxes until now. It was time to deal with this stuff. She wanted to make room for Hank.

Danielle chose me as her organizer to help her regain control of her apartment. Early on, I noticed an openness and awareness in her that made our work easier than it was with other clients, but it was still hard. We worked together two Saturdays a month. By the end of those days we were physically and mentally tired. Those unopened boxes from her marriage and move were hardest of all. At first, Danielle felt a firestorm of emotion from each box we opened. Danielle's decision making was paralyzed by anxiety, sadness, and anger. Sometimes we'd only get through a few items before it became too much for her and we had to refocus on another space for the rest of our session. Over time, working through those boxes became easier for Danielle. I thought it was because she had become more experienced in the organizing process, but then Danielle said something that changed everything.

"I told my therapist we're working on these boxes and how hard it is. When I open them, I feel everything from the divorce all over again. She's glad we're going through them though," she said as she gave a little chuckle. "It's brought up a lot for me to talk about in therapy."

Her words called to me like a siren. Our work in her home wasn't done in isolation. It was a catalyst for other aspects of her well-being. The stuff we worked on gave her stuff to talk about in therapy.

My mind raced with questions. I searched for words, but simply said, "You've been able to make decisions more quickly the last few sessions." When we first met, every decision Danielle faced needed a labored discussion about the item's memory, sentiment, and usefulness. Often, these conversations ended with Danielle saying, "I can't decide." Now, even when it was hard, she made quicker decisions and was more willing to let things go.

"Well, it makes sense, doesn't it?" Danielle said. "Therapy has helped. This," she said as she gestured to the room, "isn't just about the stuff."

Bam! That was is it!

I could help Danielle decide what to do with the cards from her bridal shower, the ceramic cake topper, and the beautiful handmade table linens her grandmother gave her as a wedding gift. The pain, regret, and sorrow surrounding her divorce, though, I couldn't help her with those feelings. But she had the support of someone who *could*. She had her therapist. The feelings and the stuff were entwined. Danielle had support to deal with both the physical stuff and the emotions it conjured. I helped her with her organizing goals, and because of our work she made great progress to move past her broken marriage. And as she made progress on her divorce in therapy, our organizing work also became easier. The two efforts complemented each other in a fluid, supportive cycle and helped Danielle find peace in both her physical and mental spaces.

This experience with Danielle shifted my approach to client work. For the first few years I accepted every client who came along, just to grow my business. I helped moms and seniors and students and everyone in between. At that time, my approach was only about the stuff: "What do you need?" "What can you let go?" These early clients often saw and felt changes in their lives, but it was rarely transformative. Some of these clients struggled with our work. Others had major relapses. Some stopped their organizing efforts before we reached their organizing goals.

Now I ask clients how they feel about their possessions and their homes and only take clients who appreciate this connection between their stuff and their emotions. They want their homes to function simply and for their belongings to have purpose and meaning. Because this approach to organizing goes beyond cute bins and neat labels, my clients don't expect a quick fix. We have longer, deeper relationships, but they also experience true transformative change. The clients who have the most success are the ones who have emotional support, whether in the form of a tight social network, a spouse, or—best yet—a therapist.

THE CYCLE OF FEELINGS AND STUFF

This book is for professionals who work with clients on mental health or emotional issues. This includes psychotherapists, psychiatrists, clinical social workers, counselors, and even life coaches. I have laid out a foundation for conversations with clients about clutter and physical space and how that aspect of their lives influences their mental health.

> *The causes of disorganization and the feelings associated with being disorganized are deeply ingrained in mental health.*

The causes of disorganization and the feelings associated with being disorganized are deeply ingrained in mental health. As shown below, when a client experiences mental health issues, this can affect their ability and motivation to maintain an orderly home. Conversely, a disorganized home can create feelings of anxiety, frustration,

The Connection Between Mental & Physical Spaces

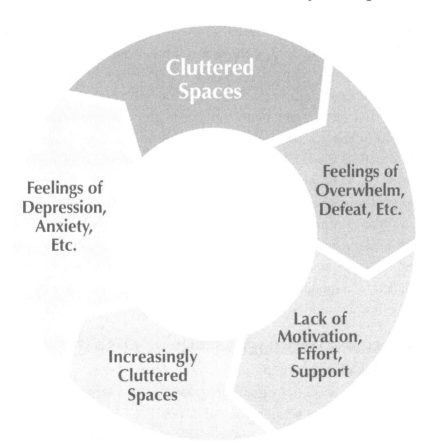

anger, sadness, and overwhelm, which can cause or exacerbate mental health troubles. In some cases, it is reasonable to assume that these two things happen simultaneously.

Therapy or professional organizing can interrupt this cycle to improve both mental health and the physical space of the home.

When I work with clients in their disorganized homes, they often express negative feelings about the state of the home in general or the items we work on specifically. When these feelings are addressed by a mental health professional, the client often has an improvement in their mental health and increased ability and motivation in their at-home organizing work.

You likely work with clients who seek help for common mental health issues such as depression, anxiety, and overwhelm. Understanding the challenges and struggles clients also experience in their physical living spaces helps to make sense of some of the underlying and consequential issues related to their mental health. Awareness of this aspect of their lives allows for another dimension to be discussed in therapy.

Organizers and therapists can partner to create a network for clients that encourages better mental health and creates a more peaceful home environment. This collaboration creates a win-win-win situation. The client reaps the benefit of two areas of their life working in conjunction with each other while being supported by two professionals. In therapy you reap the benefit of your client's newfound awareness of new emotions and triggers, which provides both great insight and the ability to spark mental health progress. And the organizer reaps the benefit of the client's emotions being handled by a qualified professional, which ultimately makes the client better prepared to tackle organizing work.

CONSIDER THE CLIENT'S PHYSICAL SPACE
It's not just about the stuff.

As a professional organizer, I work with clients when their homes are a source of stress instead of peace. Clients call when they feel overwhelmed, discouraged, sad, anxious, or confused—many of the same feelings therapy clients express. My goal is to help them simplify their lives by simplifying their physical belongings, their "stuff," and their spaces.

As I became a more experienced organizer, I realized I learned a lot about clients by seeing their stuff, but I learned even more by talking with them. At first, this was just casual banter as we worked: "How long have you lived in this house?" "Where did you go to school?" Clients spoke about weekend plans and funny family stories. The longer I worked with a client, the more personal the stories became, and they shared both the good and the bad. I heard about family drama, childhood vacations, personal regrets, stories of loss, beloved family pets—everything we touched seemed to have a story. I listened to the laughter, the screams, and many times, the tears, both happy and sad. As clients told the story of their stuff, I noticed the same comments over and over. "Why is this so hard?" "This was my mom's." "I don't know where to start."

By asking and listening, I found what I'd missed earlier in my organizing days. It wasn't just about the "stuff." The clutter in people's homes was about their *lives*. The stuff was only the physical things, tangible manifestations of memories, experiences, and feelings. I thought about the emotion held in my clients' stuff and encouraged them to think about that too. I knew I wasn't qualified to offer psychological advice, but I also knew there were questions that clients needed to ask themselves. At organizing sessions as we sorted through piles or boxes, I asked gentle questions about the item(s): "Who gave this to you?" "Why is it boxed down here instead of displayed?" "Would you miss this if we donated it?" Once the client processed the story and feelings attached to an item, objective decisions were easier to make.

By answering these questions, my clients began to experience profound, lasting change. They felt lighter physically and mentally. Addressing the stuff wasn't as daunting. They had the perspective and questions to make progress one step at a time. With practice, they started to ask themselves those gentle, probing questions: "Why is this here?" "How does this fit into my life?" This was the change I strived for—not just a change in the physical space, but a change in how they thought about their stuff.

As my focus changed to "it's not just about the stuff," people who appreciated this connection, aware of it or not, were drawn to me. Many of them were also in therapy. I found I was most successful when I worked with clients who also worked with a mental health professional, a therapist, counselor, or sometimes even a trained and qualified life coach. Some off-handedly mentioned that they were in therapy and said nothing more. With others, I knew their therapist's name, how often they met, and even what they talked about. When these clients were open with their therapists about working with an organizer, it offered the opportunity to have a conversation about a new dimension of their lives: their home space, how they felt when they were there, and how those feelings influenced their overall mental health.

The process clients used in therapy often overlapped with the process used to organize their homes. And, more specifically, some issues they worked through in therapy were also issues that came up with their physical stuff too. Connecting mental health treatment and professional organizing creates a more well-rounded approach to address not only mental health challenges, but also physical space challenges that these clients experience. And by addressing them both together they see better results, as the two worlds complement each other.

I've gone to therapy myself and appreciated the impact it had. Therapy focused on my relationships, feelings, and work. How did I feel? How did I handle this or that? How did I react to something? How could I change my thoughts and behavior in the future? The therapist guided me with pointed questions designed to process my emotions. He offered tidbits he suggested I add to my "toolbox" for when I struggled in the future. But I was never asked about my physical home. Fortunately, my home was pretty orderly, so it didn't occur to me at the time that this was an important question.

This is not to say that all clients live in homes that generate such feelings. But the relationship between the physical space and the mental state is strong enough that it deserves the ask, "Tell me about your home. How do you feel there?" These simple statements can open your awareness to a new aspect of your client's life that allows a better, more complete understanding of them.

> *"Tell me about your home. How do you feel there?" These simple statements can open a therapist's awareness to a new aspect of their client's life that allows a better, more complete understanding of them.*

Most American families and homes struggle with various levels of clutter. Many mental health professionals do not usually work inside a client's home. They may not be aware of what a client's physical home environment is like. Physical (body) health, such as weight and pallor, are seen at appointments. Mental health is the focus of treatment, but the physical space the client lives in may go unconsidered and undisclosed. Perhaps the most extreme cases (i.e., Hoarding Disorder) are brought to the attention of mental health professionals, but in lesser cases, how often is it discussed?

This book is meant to expose you, as mental health professionals, to the influence physical space has on your clients' emotional experiences in order to better understand and appreciate this connection and introduce it to clients. Then professional organizing can be used as a resource and tool to help clients reach their mental health goals.

CHAPTER 2

Organizing—Therapy's Natural Partner

JUST AS IT'S ACCEPTED THAT there's a connection between the mind and the body, there's also a connection between the mind and one's surroundings. What is the connection between stuff and emotions? What is the impact of clutter on everyday life? How does clutter impact thoughts and feelings? And does clearing physical clutter improve mental health?

All of my organizing work is with everyday people: moms and dads who both work and feel overwhelmed by the afternoon and evening chaos; the daughter who lost her mom and needs help to go through the inherited boxes; the divorced middle-age woman who has given her career the front seat but struggles with overstuffed closets. As I work with these clients, what I find most interesting is that it's very rarely ever just about the "stuff." It isn't just about the papers, the clothes, or the memorabilia. It's about their lives and what goes on in their minds!

Speaking of professional organizers (POs), Katie Kilroy-Marac, a professor of anthropology and researcher, writes:

> As POs manipulate the objects and boundaries of their clients, they aim to reorient them not just materially but also emotionally, morally, and affectively. Because they

hold as true the existence of a profound connection between the relative order or disorder of a person's domestic space and his or her state of mental health and well-being, the sorting and reordering work they do with their clients' possessions is imagined to have a similar effect on their clients' minds.[2]

Organizing physical spaces helps clients simplify one aspect of their lives. As clients see the tangible results of cleared out clutter, open space, and better organization, they have more mental energy, focus, and motivation to work on their emotions. The organizing work is focused on the space and the stuff, but the influence of these emotions can't be ignored.

In regard to these emotions, Kilroy-Marac goes on to say,

Over time, their clients open up to them - they reveal their disappointments and dreams, their dysfunctional relationships, past traumas, wishes, and fears - and these conversations often bubble up around the things that the PO and client sort through together.[3]

I experienced this firsthand with Danielle. Each box we opened brought a new wave of emotion. I recall one particular item left me fumbling for words. From one of those avoided dining room moving boxes, Danielle pulled out a large manila envelope and opened it. In an instant Danielle's face turned sad and she was in tears.

"What is it?" I asked.

"These are Charlie's adoption papers," she said through her tears. Charlie was Danielle's dog, a mid-size, lovable black mutt who was fiercely protective of Danielle. As she started to cry, as if on cue, Charlie came into the room and nuzzled under her chin to comfort her.

I was confused. Charlie wasn't a casualty of the divorce. Charlie was here with her. "Why do these make you sad?" I asked.

"I just remember getting him with Jeff. And then I thought about the day Jeff left." She paused to take a breath. "I read the note he left and fell to the floor. Charlie ran to me and I held him as I cried." Danielle sobbed. Fat tears fell onto Charlie's head. Those papers, something I thought would be a happy reminder, or at least something innocuous, pulled raw emotion from Danielle.

I was at a loss. I felt helpless and didn't know what to say. Normally, I would offer a hug or hand on the shoulder, but Danielle's embrace with Charlie seemed too intimate to intrude on. I stood there frozen as I watched Danielle cry.

Situations like this speak to the role of an organizer. The focus of organizing work is on the physical objects. A professional organizer can ask questions about the emotions and listen supportively, but is not qualified to advise or counsel on the emotions that commonly arise during organizing sessions.

The parallels between the work of mental health professionals and professional organizers, as well as the overlap in subject matter, create a natural partnership for the two fields. Organizers need therapists as partners to help clients through the range of emotions that organizing can uncover: doubt, regret, fear, overwhelm, grief, pain, anxiety, shame, embarrassment. A therapist's contribution is extremely valuable to the organizer, the client, and the organizing process. The end result is that by simultaneously working with a professional organizer and a mental health professional on both their physical and mental spaces, clients experience positive change in both.

> Organizers need therapists as partners to help clients through the range of emotions that organizing can uncover: doubt, regret, fear, overwhelm, grief, pain, anxiety, shame, embarrassment.

HOW THERAPY AND ORGANIZING ARE SIMILAR

Ryan Howes considers the relationship between therapist and client in his Psychology Today article, "Why you Lie to your Therapist." He says, "Those who make the decision to attend therapy have likely prepared themselves to invest money, time, and emotional energy in the process."[4] The same is true when the client decides to work with a professional organizer. My relationship with clients has many parallels to your relationship with your patients. Both are immensely intimate. Both span weeks, months, or possibly years. Both have variable patterns that ebb and flow. And just like each therapy patient, each organizing client and their associated experiences are strikingly unique.

Time

When clients acknowledge the role their emotions have in tackling their clutter, they realize that a quick fix or "one size fits all" organizing solution will not work. I meet with clients many times over the course of several months and, in some cases, even years. Weekly, bi-monthly, or monthly appointments are common. The organizing process takes time to learn about the client's strengths, weaknesses, preferences, habits, values, etc. Together, the client and I try different strategies, learn from past experiences, and build new methods, routines, and habits. These things all take time. Clients are also given "homework" between sessions. This may be to practice new strategies, ponder specific questions about a space so we can discuss the answers at the next session, or complete tasks that the client can accomplish on his/her own.

You meet with patients on a similar schedule, with similar goals, and similar practices. For example, you may suggest a daily meditation routine and offer tips on how to do it. Then follow up to see how it's going. What did they like? What challenges did they have? Is it something they can see themselves doing in the future? Time and a continued relationship are integral to making these incremental changes.

Intimacy

In therapy, clients open themselves to a new level of exposure and vulnerability. They speak about their experiences, thoughts, fears, insecurities, and sorrows that may not be expressed to anyone else in the world. The same is true of organizing work. Clients invite organizers into an aspect of their lives that is usually hidden from others. Have you ever been invited into someone's home and they say, "Let me show you my cluttered basement?" Of course not! But organizers are invited into this intimate space every day.

Intimacy is evident from the very first in-home meeting with new clients, the assessment. At the assessment, we do a walkthrough of the house before we sit down to make an action plan. I always tell the client, "Do not clean up before I come!" This is the best way for me to truly understand the struggles that the client has.

When I entered Joann's home for her assessment, she immediately shook her head and said, "I'm so sorry for the mess. This is embarrassing."

"Nothing to be embarrassed about. You needed help, so you called. This is what I do," I reassured her.

We toured her modest home and came to a corner in her bedroom that held an eclectic collection: laundry baskets filled with papers, bags, toys, and clothes; shopping bags with receipts, picture frames, a soccer ball, a reusable shopping bag, and a six-pack of bottled water; two pieces of luggage; and various other things.

"Tell me about these things here," I said.

"We had company the other night so this is everything I cleaned up from the living room," she replied. "We were in a hurry, so everything just got shoved here."

"Once things land here, is there a plan for them so they get put away?" I asked.

Joann grinned and chuckled with embarrassment. "No, they stay here and even more will get added to it the next time we have company and have to clean up again. This is the problem. Nothing ever gets done and I feel like a failure about it. I hate seeing this every time I'm in here," she said, disgusted.

There is anxiety, or even shame, in homes being less than perfect or, heaven forbid, lived in. For clients, this part of their lives, a part that is commonly hidden from others, is a persistent visual reminder of feelings of doubt, frustration, sorrow, anger, and overwhelm. It is a very vulnerable moment to show that to a stranger and ask for help. Over time, the intimacy of the work and the relationship both deepen as the organizer becomes a trusted resource. More than just a guide through their stuff, the organizer is often the person in the room to offer a hug, a word of encouragement, or a push forward. This is all delicately balanced with remaining professional, watching the clock, and staying positive.

> *More than just a guide through their stuff, the organizer is often the person in the room to offer a hug, a word of encouragement, or a push forward.*

Confidentiality

Of course, any truly *professional* professional organizer follows a code of ethics that protects the privacy and confidentiality of clients. Some clients sign disclosures to allow the use of either their words or photos of their spaces as a testimony of the work. This, however, should always be optional and rescindable at any time. Everything except what has been given explicit permission to share is kept in strict confidence. Trusted organizers never share whom they work with, what their clients' homes look like, or what is seen in those homes. Just as your clients trust you to respect their privacy and confidentiality, an organizer's commitment to these allows clients to feel confident in their privacy and allows them to be open in the experience.

Variability

Perhaps the most striking similarity between the fields is the variability in clients' progress. In both therapy and engaged organizing, clients do not move in a straight line from start to finish. Their goals include an improvement in mental health or their physical space. This is the upward trend clients work toward. However, day-to-day, they make small gains, have setbacks, sometimes reach a new peak, and sometimes plateau. These daily patterns show the variability of their progress over time. This variability has value since it allows clients to move at their own pace and accounts for life's circumstances and the individual's own goals. It can also be a challenge when setbacks or plateaus occur. When clients expect this variability in their progress, they can set more realistic expectations of themselves and the process.

Uniqueness

Although there are standard therapy practices, each client has their own unique circumstances, needs, and expectations. And each client sees results at different times and with different outcomes.

Each organizing client is also a unique blend of personality, commitment, and worldview. These things influence the organizing process just as much as the space and what's in it. Some clients are quick to make decisions, while others need more time to ponder. Some clients experience greater sentimental attachment. Some clients want printed, color coded labels for every bin, while others just want to be able to see the floor. None of these ways are right or wrong. It is part of the process for the organizer to learn about the client and suggest options that fit the client's personality and lifestyle.

Of course, there many ways that organizing and therapy differ, but in these ways—time, intimacy, confidentiality, variability, and uniqueness—they are similar. While the focuses of the two fields are different, these parallels show how the two fields complement each other. Clients may be more open to use both of these services when they understand the likenesses they share. For organizers, it is important to have a basic understanding of the therapeutic process, common techniques, and strategies. Conversely, understanding the world of organizing and clutter helps you appreciate the role professional organizers play in clients' homes.

CHAPTER 3

Clutter in Context: What is Clutter?

TO UNDERSTAND THE ROLE of a professional organizer, it is helpful to know what they do. In the simplest and most obvious way, their goal is to eliminate the clutter and disorganization from clients' lives. But what are clutter and organization? How are they defined?

Clutter

In their academic paper, "The Dark Side of Home: Assessing possession 'clutter' on subjective well-being," Drs. Catherine Roster, Joseph Ferrari, and M. Peter Jurkat define clutter as "an overabundance of possessions that collectively create chaotic and disorderly living spaces."[5] All the stuff that is out of place or doesn't have a "home," in organizing lingo, is physical clutter. Clutter can differ in size and content: from piles of paper on the desk, to a jumble of toys on the floor, to coats that hang on the backs of chairs, to the boxes and boxes of stuff in the garage or basement or storage unit.

An even simpler definition of clutter comes from Barbara Hemphill's book *Taming the Paper Tiger at Home.* Hemphill simply says, "Clutter is postponed decisions."[6] Clutter happens when you don't know what to do with something, so instead of deciding, you put it down, put it aside, or box it up. It can seem too overwhelming, unimportant, or time or energy consuming to make a decision about what should be done with a particular item. Things often get put down "for now" to be dealt with "later." Over time, these delayed decisions accumulate and create a clutter problem.

> Clutter happens when you don't know what to do with something, so instead of deciding, you put it down, put it aside, or box it up.

Clutter becomes a problem when it affects the use of a space. A space can be one particular area of a room, say the countertops of the kitchen, an entire room, or any combination of rooms.

The stuff is a bit harder to define since it is different for everyone. Stuff, clutter, and disorganization are all the things that cause feelings of disarray, frustration, or disappointment. Stuff becomes a problem when it impedes the health, safety, and happiness of its owner. This can be a direct result of the physical things or the indirect result of the *feelings* associated with those things.

These definitions focus on physical clutter, but there is mental clutter as well. Mental clutter is all that stuff that bounces around in the mind. Just like physical clutter, mental clutter can be small—keeping track of schedules and important dates, figuring out what you need to buy while you walk through the grocery store, trying to remember where you put your keys—or big—doubts, regrets, insecurities, etc. On the whole, mental clutter shows itself in poor time management, trouble prioritizing, or trouble making decisions.

Organization

The most common definition of "organized" is to be able to find what you need when you need it. The beauty of this simple definition is it allows for latitude and subjectivity. Just as with the definition of clutter, organization can look very different to one person than it does to another. The needs of each person vary, and therefore the organization systems implemented are unique to them as well. Organizing solutions are designed to take into account a person's habits, routines, and preferences. The needs of an artist are very different from the needs of a young family, which are very different from the needs of a small business entrepreneur who works from home. What makes each of these people organized is whether or not their space functions so that they can find what they need when they need it. If each can, then there is organization. When they can't find what they need when they need it, that is when they experience disorganization.

> The most common definition of "organized" is to be able to find what you need when you need it.

Subjectivity of Space and Stuff

Interestingly, these definitions of clutter and organization are largely subjective. They look different to everyone. For some, the stuff is a basement full of boxes inherited from a deceased parent. For others, the stuff will be the leftovers that accumulate from daily living such as unfinished laundry and unopened mail left to be put away later. Still others may define stuff as closets that have gradually accumulated clothes that no longer fit, function, or flatter. Or it can be a combination of any or all of these.

The influence of clutter is also very personal and subjective. Everyone has a different threshold for his or her clutter tolerance. Some people find clutter extremely distracting or angst producing, while others can largely ignore it. And yes, these different views are a breeding ground for conflict. Spouses, parents and children, or siblings disagree over whose stuff creates the clutter, who is responsible for it, or how a room should look.

My husband Luke and I had a firsthand encounter with opposing views of clutter. After the birth of our second daughter, Luke graciously gave up his home office so it could become the nursery. This meant that Luke and I would share my office. Since we both often worked from home, we each would spend a fair amount of time in this newly joined space.

From the outset I knew our styles would be hard to combine.

His old office had a cozy feel, painted a dark brown with navy accents. He situated his desk inside a black armoire that he repurposed so his desk could convert for sitting or standing. Stacks of papers to read and process seemed to infinitely collect on his desk. Not to mention the random things there as well: the watch that needed a new battery, his checkbook, and opened but unprocessed pieces of mail. To me, his desk looked more like a catchall spot than a place of work and productivity.

I was the polar opposite. I liked white space and room to breathe. My office was painted a lovely shade of light grey with furniture that was all white and beechwood tones. Papers were corralled nightly into an inbox so that the desk's surface was a blank slate each morning. Everything was contained and neatly labeled. Floor-length curtains of soft fabric covered the window. I even took down the stark closet doors and replaced them with floor-length curtains to soften the room. This was a place of focus, clear surfaces, and clean lines. This was a tranquil place to work.

It only took a few days for the clash to begin. Luke's black desk stood out like a sore thumb against the soft hues of the room. The beautiful curtains were left haphazardly open whenever he went into the closet. The stacks of paper and random stuff on Luke's desk grabbed my attention every single time I walked into the room. *Why does he need so much stuff out?* I thought every time I saw his "cluttered" desk.

But according to the definition of organized, Luke was. Those papers? That was the current assignment from his students that he was grading. The opened mail? The things he needed to write checks for, and that was why his checkbook was there. He used his desk as a processing center, and that worked for him. He knew exactly what was on his desk. To me, it looked like chaos. To him, it was organized. Ironically, he said to me about my desk, "How do you ever know what you are supposed to be working on if you put everything away every night? It's like you have to start over every day. Isn't that a waste of time?"

Our different comfort levels for an acceptable amount of "clutter" created conflict. Neither of us was right or wrong. We just had different interpretations of clutter and disorganization because of their subjectivity. I'd like to say we compromised, but we didn't. We knew it was best if we didn't share an office anymore and, thankfully, Luke relocated his workspace elsewhere.

This subjectivity means that there is no "one size fits all" solution for clutter. There is no right or wrong way to be organized or a "right" amount of stuff in a space. There are great tips and common strategies, but personal preferences and circumstances must be considered too.

In that important article, "The Dark Side of Home," the authors touch on an even more critical reality. It's not just about the stuff. A physically cluttered and disorganized home has a profound effect on mental health.[7] The stuff—the clutter in our homes—creates and influences an environment of chaos. Anyone's home space should be a place that aids in the functioning of life, an escape from the outside world. When the effects of clutter begin to have an influence on mental health, clients are better served by professionals who understand clutter and disorganization, have knowledge of the connection between physical and mental spaces, and have the tools to guide them to make positive changes in both their physical and mental worlds.

> *A physically cluttered and disorganized home has a profound effect on mental health.*

Regarding Hoarding Disorder

Often, the work of professional organizers conjures images of hoarded homes. The attention the industry receives from shows such as *Hoarding: Buried Alive* and *Hoarders* isn't an accurate representation of the majority of organizing work. Many initial calls from clients start with them saying, "I'm not a hoarder." Contrary to television depictions, for many POs hoarding is a small, if any, portion of their work. Yes, some professional organizers work in hoarding situations, but many don't.

Hoarding Disorder (HD) is a complex situation that needs the attention of therapists, organizers, and support services trained to address both the physical and mental components of the diagnosis. There are even neurological components that have been identified in hoarding disorder.[8] In its DSM-5 classification, three of the key components of HD are:

1. Persistent difficulty discarding or parting with possessions, regardless of their actual value

2. A perceived need to save the items and to the distress associated with discarding them.

3. Accumulation of possessions that congest and clutter active living areas and substantially compromises their intended use. If living areas are uncluttered, it is only because of the interventions of third parties (e.g., family members, cleaners, authorities).[9]

It is in these components where most organizing clients and those with HD differ. In Hoarding Disorder, there is acquisition of items, but the real trouble lies in their difficulty to let things go and the distress they experience when they part with things. Those with Hoarding Disorder "are significantly less likely than friends or family members to view their living situations as a problem and are resistant to treatment efforts, which can create frustration and escalate tensions."[10] Those POs properly trained in chronic disorganization and Hoarding Disorder are an amazing asset in these situations, and offer the hands-on, in-home help needed.

My clients feel differently, however, because they *want* to let go. As they make decisions and discard items, they feel motivated, lighter, and inspired. They may need guidance to help them find their best answers, but when they dispose, lessen, and declutter, the experience is positive and exhilarating.

HD clients have different goals and different strategies are needed to meet them. It is because of this difference that the concepts, ideas, and strategies I offer in this book are not meant for hoarding situations.

CHAPTER 4

The Work of Professional Organizers

TODAY, IN TERMS OF WELLNESS, we often think of the mind/body connection. Eastern medicine, scientific study, and experiential evidence support the connection between the mind and the body. As a professional organizer, this connection envelops another dimension: physical surroundings. As clients purge, sort, organize, and systematize their physical possessions, they experience the mental clarity and ease that dealing with their stuff brings. But what exactly is a professional organizer? And, how does professional organizing relate to the mental health field?

In her academic paper, "A Magical Reorientation of the Modern: Professional Organizers and Thingly Care in Contemporary North America," Katie Kilroy-Marac said professional organizers "described their work [...] as coaching, acting as a sounding board, lending focus, setting goals, teaching, transferring skills, modeling behavior, acting as a mirror, and helping clients establish new habits."[11]

The concept of helping others organize as a profession was formalized in the mid-1980s with the creation of the National Association of Professional Organizers (NAPO), now branded as the National Association of Productivity and Organizing Professionals (still NAPO). Professional organizers work with their clients to help them clear out clutter, create or improve systems for productivity, and manage their resources so the client can live their most simple and enjoyable life.

Although often dramatized, the majority of professional organizing work focuses on very ordinary homes. Kilroy-Marac notes this as well:

> It's not just the extreme cases of acquisition, accumulation, or excess that POs find interesting or worthy of discussion, but also the mundane, ordinary things that settle into our daily lives - the paper clutter (receipts, tax documents, letters, junk mail), the plastic goods, the useless kitchen gadgets, the kids' artwork, the new-but-soon-to-be-obsolete electronic devices, and the things we inherit when a parent or loved one dies.[12]

Services can be divided into residential and business. Residential organizers help individuals and families with their home living spaces. Business organizers help employees, executives, or even whole companies create systems for productivity, efficiency, or resource management.

PHYSICAL SPACES

My specialty is residential organizing. I work with clients in their homes from basements to attics, closets to playrooms, kitchens to dens, paperwork to memorabilia. My goal is to simplify life for my clients by simplifying their space. A simplified home gives them less stress, less conflict, less to maintain, more time, more money, and more space. Through the process, clients discover what items they want, need, and use in their homes and eliminate the rest. Habits and systems are developed to help them achieve their goals, even if that is to simply leave the house on time without searching for anyone's missing shoe.

The tangible nature of working on physical stuff is significant because clients can immediately see results. When a client "needs a win" to create or sustain motivation, seeing a freshly cleared space, even if it is just one shelf or drawer, can be extremely rewarding.

I worked with Pam, a married stay-at-home mom with four kids. Although her family lived in a nice-sized house, she called because her home felt stressful. The closets were stuffed, the playroom was in a constant state of chaos, and her dining room table was the drop zone catch-all for anything coming into or going out of the house. She felt frazzled as she tried to find things, the kids constantly fought about left out toys, and a lot of money was spent on duplicate purchases since buying something again was easier than trying to find the one they already owned. Pam and I purged the excess, created easy to maintain systems, and simplified processes so these spaces in her home could function with more ease, less thought, and less stress. After our work, toys were easily found and easily put away. Spending decreased since things had labeled homes so Pam knew exactly what she had. And best of all, Pam felt lighter in her home, which had more open space and fewer stressors. This is the work of residential professional organizers, helping clients find that calm within their homes.

PRODUCTIVITY AND TIME MANAGEMENT

POs work with clients on productivity and time management even in residential settings. The current American lifestyle is one of consumption, busyness, and distraction. This can often mean that individuals and families feel like they are in a hamster wheel, constantly on the go, but not getting ahead.

Whether in a home or work environment, productivity and time management are crucial skills. These skills allow clients to work smarter instead of harder. In homes, this means streamlined systems and better routines. This can be meal planning and once a week food shopping, a laundry and/or cleaning routine, or daily maintenance habits. Creating these systems encourages better use of energy and resources—which, in many homes, are already in short supply.

Stan called because he wanted to improve his productivity. He struggled with a backlog of work on his desk. He worked three days a week with clients at his business location and two days a week from home on his administrative work. I was surprised when Stan showed me his desk area set up in his living room. I expected piles of paper and disorder, but other than on the top of his desk, I didn't see many papers.

"I'm really good with scanning and filing things once they're done," Stan explained. "It's the actually getting things done that I struggle with. I never know what to work on next and am always afraid that something will fall through the cracks. I'm a morning person. I'm up at 5:00 a.m. and jump right in to work. I start with my email," Stan told me. "But every day is different after that. I tend to work on whatever is most important. If something is important, I'll put it on top of my computer, so I'm sure to see it first."

I looked at Stan's computer and saw several pieces of mail, scrawled notes, and files piled on top of his closed laptop. "So, all of this is important? How do you decide what to do first from this pile?" I asked.

He picked up the first piece of paper and said, "Well, I put this on top since it's due tomorrow. So, I would start with this."

"How about new tasks or papers that come in? What do you do with those?" I asked.

"Papers just go into a pile until I look at them. Most things come to me digitally so that doesn't get too bad. And Jen, my assistant, works from home so she texts me questions as they come up. I try to get back to her right away, so I don't hold her up. If she needs me to do something, I put it on a sticky note on my desk to remind me to do it. I even do that, write a note, if I think of something I need to work on or something comes up in an email."

"Do the reminders work well for you?" I asked, straight-faced, as I looked at the sticky notes that covered the surface of his desk, in some spots two or three notes deep.

Stan chuckled at the question and at himself. "No," he said with a grin, "they do not."

Stan's admin days were busy, but they weren't efficient. He confused what was important with what was urgent. Everything became urgent if it was due tomorrow! Stan was distracted by what was right in front of him—both literally and figuratively.

Stan and I got to work to revamp his productivity. He was tech savvy and liked the idea of using his computer to create order. In contrast to his desk, his computer files were all neatly labeled, ordered, and searchable. One concern, though, was that he thought he would forget about his reminders if they weren't out in front of him. We talked about a few different task management platforms he could use on his computer. He particularly liked one option that allowed him to collaborate virtually with Jen on projects and tasks. He assigned each task a priority level and a due date, and the app pushed notifications to him on his phone.

Then we implemented a schedule to work on those tasks. Stan had high energy in the morning, but wasted that peak time on mundane things like email. Instead, we blocked off two hours at the start of each admin day for tasks that took a lot of mental energy like writing proposals and drafting designs. Later in the mornings he checked the task management software. He sorted tasks by due date and/or priority to decide what needed to be worked on next. Finally, he processed email in the afternoon, a perfect time for that routine and mundane task that required less mental energy. With better use of his time, Stan was more productive and able to get ahead on tasks instead of focusing just on what was due next.

MOVE MANAGEMENT, CLEAN OUTS, AND ESTATE SALES

Organizing and project management skills apply to various other services as well. For example, POs are called in to work on large scale clean outs of homes. Perhaps the home is part of an estate that is being settled or owned by a couple preparing to downsize.

As with many clients, Sue and Alan's accumulation of things was gradual over many years. They lived in the same split-level home for thirty years as they grew from young couple to working professionals to retirees. Through the years they enjoyed many stages of life and hobbies. Each came with its corresponding "stuff." As avid travelers who visited nearly every corner of the world, they had clothing and equipment for every kind of adventure: jungle safaris, city walking tours, mountain hiking, and island-wear. From every new location visited they brought back mementos and reminders of their travels. They were both only children, so when their parents passed, Sue and Alan became the keepers of many family items and relics like photographs and furniture passed down from generation to generation. Their hobbies also garnered many other collected things: prized record albums, comic books, scrapbooking supplies, camping equipment, and artwork.

For Sue and Alan, the default whenever something needed to be cleaned up or put away was to put it in the garage. They were fortunate to have an oversized two-car garage, but it was so full there was no room to park! The garage had become the resting place for all the things they didn't know what else to do with. It seemed manageable to them until a home renovation brought several more items and boxes into the garage. That's when Sue called me.

"Once the renovation is done, I don't want to put all this junk back into the house. But I also don't want it living here either," Sue said of the stuffed garage. "But what do you do with this stuff? I don't even know how to get rid of it!"

We worked together to purge, sort, and organize the contents of the garage. We found lots of interesting things like an ancestor's birth certificate from eastern Europe dated back to the 1800s, three unmatched skis, boxes of costume jewelry, and a full-size, jeweler-grade, two-thousand-pound safe. (This, however, was thankfully empty.)

We discarded the trash, donated the useful, and brought in a professional company to do an estate sale of the valuable. Our sorting meant we had categories of items that were easily allocated into lots. Sue and Alan made a sizable amount of money from the estate sale, which covered the cost of my services and the estate sale fees. All the stuff in the garage was dealt with and they could park inside it! How novel!

Another valuable service is to coordinate and manage residential moves. This goes well beyond simply unboxing the packed items. A team of skilled professional organizers can unpack a new home for immediate, intuitive use. Organizers know the common and practical setups for bathrooms, kitchens, and closets so homes can be up and running quickly and efficiently.

> *By bringing hands-on project management skills to clients, organizers help ease transitions, events, and life in a variety of circumstances and situations.*

POs can also introduce you to important resources for clients. As in-home professionals, organizers know about associations such as the Institute for Challenging Disorganization, The National Association of Senior Move Managers, and the Association of Personal Photo Organizers, and often give referrals for real estate agents, handymen, plumbers, electricians, and house cleaners.

There are corresponding specialties for POs, such as senior move managers, photo organizers, daily money managers, and financial organizers, who each serve various markets of clients. Some organizers work with chronic disorganization, ADHD clients, families, students, or those going through a life transition. The combination of services offered and types of clients is numerous. By bringing hands-on project management skills to clients, organizers help ease transitions, events, and life in a variety of circumstances and situations.

PART 2

The Connection

"*[Professional organizers] operate within a realm of magical correspondence where matter and mind are imagined to reflect and affect one another, and where bringing order to a client's possessions means also bringing order to his or her mind.*"[13]
— KATIE KILROY-MARAC

CHAPTER 5

The Mental/Physical Clutter Connection

MODERN CULTURE AND SCIENTIFIC MEDICINE acknowledge the mind-body connection. The next step is to consider the mind-environment connection. How do the mind and environment interrelate and influence each other? And once the connection is understood, how can organizers and therapists alter their approaches to use this connection to their client's advantage?

> *How do the mind and environment interrelate and influence each other?*

Whenever I give a talk on the connection between physical and mental spaces, I ask the audience to think about the weather. Most of the attendees are mental health professionals in the Northeast who experience hot, humid summers and cold, snowy winters.

"Tell me how you feel in mid-winter, let's say late January," I ask the crowd. "The days are shorter. The temperature is lower. There might be snow on the ground. How does that season make you feel?"

The answers are always similar, called out in low, dreary tones to emphasize the feelings: "Tired." "Lazy." "Unmotivated." "Sad." "Lethargic." "Not enough time."

"Now how do you feel in mid-summer, July. The days are longer. The temperature is higher. It might be hazy and humid. How does that season make you feel?" I'm always very careful about the words I use in these examples to describe the seasons. The days are shorter or longer. The temperature is lower or higher. Snow and humidity are normal conditions in these northeastern seasons. I even watch my tone of voice in order to not allow my personal opinions to sway their answers.

I can almost see the happiness on their faces as they consider the warm summer weather. They call out with enthusiasm: "Alive!" "Energized!" "Happy!"

What influences those feelings? In both seasons we have the same jobs, live in the same houses, have bills to pay and responsibilities to fulfill. What is different? The weather. The outside physical environment changes, and that changes how we feel! In winter we feel weighed down, tired. In summer we feel lighter and more energized.

The natural environment influences personal mood and feelings. The constructed environment, the home, does as well. When this most intimate place, the home, is cluttered, it creates an emotional reaction too.

DANIELLE REVISITED

Danielle was the first client who sparked an interest in me to learn more about the symbiotic relationship between organizing and therapy. Danielle's home was cluttered from the entryway to the kitchen, and all the way to the bedroom. Danielle and her new boyfriend, Hank, talked about his moving in with her and that was the inspiration for Danielle to tackle her clutter. If Hank moved in, and brought his stuff with him, she needed and wanted to make space for him.

At the assessment, Danielle said things I hear many times over from my clients: "I don't know where to begin." "I feel overwhelmed." "I should be able to do this on my own, but I just can't." But Danielle went a step further. She was very open with me about being in therapy. In therapy, she talked about her depression, anxiety, heartbreaking divorce, and her struggle with negative self-talk. "My therapist and I have talked about the wedding and divorce, but I still have these boxes of wedding stuff that I haven't been able to go through. I've tried to keep my closet organized, but when I don't, I get mad at myself. I know that isn't fair to do that, but it's hard to avoid when I see this every day. It's been like this since I was a kid. I always had a messy room." The clincher for me was when Danielle said, "I avoid being home because I don't like how I feel here." My heart ached. Home should be a place to escape to, not from!

But Danielle knew that it was about more than the "stuff." What about all the feelings she had about her belongings and her space? Those were intricately woven into her experience of her things. Decisions were hard because they involved sentiment, grief, and anxiety. She could work on those feelings in therapy, but they had a different cadence when faced with physical, tactile objects that elicited powerful emotions.

Danielle, Hank, and I started to organize their soon-to-be shared home. We took small steps and talked a lot. Danielle explained the emotional attachments she felt. I listened and tried to suggest solutions that respected her feelings while also moved her toward her goal of a renewed space that felt like a home, a place to escape to instead of from.

The change I saw in Danielle's home and life over the course of our work was amazing. As we worked through her physical space, Danielle shared the stories of her things and shared laughter, tears, regrets, fond memories, and not-so-fond memories. Danielle brought each of these stories and feelings to her therapist for them to work on there. And the results were transformative. As we tackled her "stuff," she had new things to talk through in therapy. And as she worked through them in therapy, she found it easier to work through the physical stuff at home. At each of our organizing sessions Danielle had more clarity, focus, and decisiveness. She felt better at home as her space transformed and some of her depression, anxiety, and overwhelm eased. She worked on her physical space and her mental space simultaneously and experienced improvement in both.

THE INFLUENCE OF CLUTTER AND FEELINGS

The weather example and Danielle's story show the interaction between physical space and mental state. People experience an emotional reaction to surroundings, environment, and things. A cluttered home can make a client feel negatively about herself, which makes it harder for her to make changes. In some cases, this can result in even more clutter and it becomes cyclical.

Everyday Clutter

For Danielle, and in most cluttered homes, there are two levels of disorganization. First, Danielle had everyday clutter. She struggled with laundry that didn't get put away, mail that collected at the front door, papers left out, and shoes that piled up. Every home has its own versions of everyday clutter. Personally, this is shoes, coats, and book bags that pile near the garage door or the miscellaneous to-do items that are put on my desk as reminders. Everyday clutter is a by-product of the living that is done in a space.

Although common, this everyday clutter creates feelings. Misplaced keys cause frustration. A piece of lost mail fuels a heated argument with a spouse. There is anger about having to make room on counters to do tasks like prepare dinner. Cheeks flush with embarrassment if an unexpected visitor arrives. These are all familiar feelings. They are understandable, expected, and the result of relatively minor occurrences. In general, adults take these things in stride and move past them. But when these feelings become more frequent, intense, and troubling, they can result in a more stressful home life or, more positively, a catalyst for change.

Accumulated Clutter

Over time, clutter accrues to the second level of disorganization, accumulated clutter. This includes items that one gathers, boxes, and/or stores away to deal with "later." Later can mean tomorrow, next year, or never. Danielle experienced this accumulated clutter too. Her closets were overfull with clothes in different sizes and from different stages of her life. (We did have some fun as we purged the clubbing clothes from her twenties!) Filing cabinets were stuffed with papers and information collected over the years. And, of course, there were those boxes from her divorce that she brought to her new home and never opened. My own basement has bins of hand-me-downs that I save for our younger daughter and boxes of photographs we inherited from my mother-in-law; things that are saved for tomorrow and from yesterday, respectively.

Accumulated clutter results from the constant influx of new things without conscientious outflow. As life happens, it is often easier to squirrel things away and let them fill closets, basements, and attics. This clutter leaks into garages, sheds, and "extra" rooms of the house. Perhaps there is even an offsite storage unit. Usually, this is the result of the common passing of time. Children's clothes and toys get packed away. House project leftovers are saved "just in case." New purchases are made. Memorabilia is boxed. It is easier to box things up and put them aside than face the difficult and time-consuming task of deciding about them. When, often years later, clients go through these boxes, they say things like, "I don't know why I saved this," or, "I didn't even know this was here."

> *Accumulated clutter results from the constant influx of new things without conscientious outflow.*

So full, these spaces can be too overwhelming to tackle. Clients may feel disappointed that they allowed this much clutter to build up, overwhelmed by the volume of stuff or intimidated by the process of clearing it out. They may doubt their ability to do it themselves or feel defeated by the prospect of that project.

		Physical	Mental
Types of Clutter	Everyday	Misplaced keys Lost mail Shuffling items to "make room" Cluttered surfaces	Frustration Conflict Anger Embarrassment Stress
	Accumulated	Stuffed closets Storage Units Accumulation of items in basements and/or attic Ineffective/inefficient use of space	Overwhelm Defeat Anger Stress Doubt Guilt

Mental Influence

The influence of home is just one side of the equation. The corresponding mental side is equally important. Yes, clutter can create and influence feelings, but feelings can also create clutter. Clients' feelings of overwhelm, depression, anxiety, and guilt influence the choices made about their surroundings. If a client experiences depression, for example, he may not have the motivation, mental energy, or physical energy for upkeep of his home. As these feelings occur more frequently with the same resulting actions, clutter accumulates.

> *Yes, clutter can create and influence feelings,*
> *but feelings can also create clutter.*

When Danielle looked into her closet, she felt anxious and

stressed. Because of how she felt, she avoided putting away fresh-ly washed clothes. The stress and anxiety Danielle experienced de-creased her motivation to do such ordinary tasks—which created more clutter.

The larger areas of clutter, such as basements and attics, or sit-uations where clutter has become intrusive in multiple areas of the home, can also have deep rooted feelings. Overwhelm can paralyze someone to the point of avoidance. Fear of making the wrong deci-sions may prevent a client from getting started.

Even the process of getting organized can be emotional. The mom client feels taken advantage of since she constantly picks up after her children and spouse. The elderly couple regrets that they have to downsize. The corporate woman feels shame that her home is a mess. It is not just about the stuff. It is about the emotion at-tached to the stuff, the mere idea of the stuff, or the process of letting go. Emotions can prevent clients from dealing with the clutter in their physical space. People feel stuck. They don't know how to start or what to do, both physically and mentally.

CYCLICAL NATURE
AND BENEFIT OF WORKING ON BOTH

The relationship between mental state and physical space is comple-mentary since each influences the other. A joint approach disturbs the negative cycle and creates a positive one. Through their work, both organizers and therapists can interrupt this cycle at any point. As the physical space is cleared, it creates a clearer mental space. The clearer mental space allows for progress in the physical space. The two, mental state and physical space, work in tandem together.

The two, mental state and physical space,
work in tandem together.

When physical space is addressed, clients begin to feel better, both in their homes and about themselves. As their homes become less cluttered, they begin to reap the mental and emotional benefits of less stress, less conflict, and less guilt than their previously cluttered home caused. Their physical space becomes less stressful and they have the ability to move beyond everyday stressors to address deeper mental health issues.

When mental health issues are addressed, clients are better prepared to work on their physical spaces. They are more open to letting physical things go and show greater motivation and optimism. They are more empowered to make positive and proactive decisions about physical things in the future. By providing guidance and support through mental health services and professional organizing, therapists and organizers can jointly help clients create an environment for positive and lasting change.

CHAPTER 6

The Psychology of Stuff

WHAT MAKES A HOUSE A HOME? It's more than the physical space. Homes are a reflection of one's self and act as a place of privacy and security. Each home has its own style, feel, and energy. Homes even have their own unique smell. There is more to a house than what physical characteristics it has or what possessions are inside it. The sense of "home" is crafted by the mind instead of tactile things.

HOUSE VS. (PSYCHOLOGICAL) HOME

I saw academic researcher Dr. Joseph Ferrari at a conference on challenging disorganization. He spoke about this sense of home:

> If you are in a family that moves around a lot as a child and you live in many places, perhaps part of a military family, you have many houses, but you still understand and know what 'home' is. If you lose your house to a fire you don't call yourself 'houseless,' but instead 'homeless.'[14]

Dr. Ferrari, along with his co-authors Catherine Roster and M. Peter Jurkat, delved into the deeper meaning of "home" in "The Dark Side of Home: Assessing possession 'clutter' on subjective well-being."[15] They revealed home to be, "not only a physical place, but also a vital source of meaning, belonging, and identity." Together, these create the "psychological home." *This* is the feeling that is created by more than the walls, floors, and doors.

The psychological home has three main functions:

1. Mental refuge from the external world by providing security, privacy, and protection
2. Attachments to objects that support self-identity
3. Greater psychological well-being.[16]

Psychological home is the space for safety and respite. It is where you keep those items that express who you are and where you feel good. This is the purpose of this most intimate environment. However, when a home is cluttered and/or disorganized (knowing that these are subjective terms), this psychological home is threatened. As Roster, Ferrari, and Jurkat write, "Excessively cluttered physical environments can cause people to feel entrapped, not only physically, but also psychologically, in declining physical environments that undermine the person's sense of self and his or her relationships with others."[17]

> *"Excessively cluttered physical environments can cause people to feel entrapped, not only physically, but also psychologically. . ."*

One cannot find refuge from the external world when the home is a source of tension and frustration. Self-identity cannot be supported when the surrounding stuff is overwhelming, intrusive, or daunting. Optimal well-being is not possible when this intimate space is an added stressor.

Their article went on to look at the connections between clutter and well-being and the results were insightful. First, the authors found that clutter had a direct negative impact on a person's subjective well-being. Clutter made participants feel bad about themselves. Recall Danielle said, "I get mad at myself," and, "I should be able to do this on my own." These are common comments from clients when they talk about their clutter and homes.

Next, clutter negatively affected the psychological home—that feeling of security and safety. Clutter minimized the sanctity of home. When cluttered, home was a place of tension, stress, and conflict, the opposite of how home should feel.

And finally, the psychological home correlated with subjective well-being. A stronger feeling of psychological home supported positive thoughts about oneself. When a home was cluttered, the psychological home was jeopardized. This negative effect on psychological home indirectly decreased subjective well-being.[18]

These aspects of mental health, subjective well-being and the psychological home, are strengthened by taking control of clutter. This is the work of professional organizers who have the tools and expertise to reduce, manage, and overcome clutter. By teaching these skills to clients, organizers give them the ability to create change in their physical space and reap the related mental health benefits.

STRESS

Stress and *stressful* are the most common words used to describe the effects of clutter and disorganization. Prolonged stress is harmful to the human body. Cortisol, also known as the stress hormone, measures stress. Cortisol levels have a normal pattern of peaks and drops throughout the day. These peaks of cortisol are needed for everyday functioning.[19] For example, cortisol helps us to wake up in the morning, regulate blood sugar, and reduce inflammation. Stress also causes cortisol levels to rise and puts the body into "high alert" mode. This is a good thing when there is an immediate threat to safety or well-being. It was an evolutionary necessity. Drops in cortisol levels are equally important, as they allow the body to recover from stressful events. However, prolonged states of stress cause cortisol to remain spiked, and human bodies are not designed to sustain stress and peaked cortisol levels over long periods of time.

Clutter is so prevalent that 84 percent of Americans feel their homes aren't organized enough, and 55 percent of them say that this disorganization is a cause of stress.[20]

Influence of Clutter on Mental Well-Being

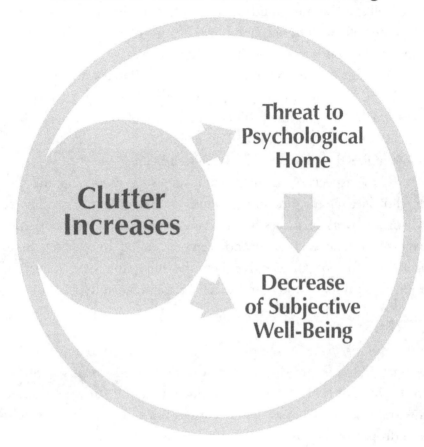

Clutter itself is stressful. It represents all that is avoided and undecided. Remember, the simplest definition of clutter is "delayed decisions." Clutter causes frustration with the living environment. The home doesn't feel peaceful or relaxing—a threat to the psychological home. This clutter and disorganization often cause conflict between family members within the home. Think of any argument that stems from someone not being able to find something important or from tripping over someone else's left out shoes. These facets of clutter feed off of each other. Frustration with the space also causes short temperedness and leads to conflict. The emotional drain of conflict reduces mental and emotional energy to address the physical clutter. It becomes cyclical.

> *This clutter and disorganization often cause conflict between family members within the home.*

In a 2010 study published in the article, "No Place Like Home: Home Tours Correlate with Daily Patterns of Mood and Cortisol" researchers, Darby Saxbe and Rena Repetti, looked at the effects of perception of home on cortisol levels. By testing cortisol, they had a quantitative measure of the stress that participants felt in their own homes.[21]

These researchers measured how often thirty families used "stressful" words versus "restorative" words to describe their homes and compared these results to cortisol levels. One of the most widely used self-reported words in this study by participants was "mess."[22]

3-Fold Impact of Clutter on Stress

STRESSFUL VS. RESTORATIVE WORDS

Stressful	Restorative
Messy	Relaxed
Junk	Calm
Clutter	Soothing
Overflowing	Lounge
Sloppy	Homey
Trash	Hangout
Unfinished	Nature

Their results indicated trouble for women in particular. When women used more stressful words to describe their homes, cortisol levels fluctuated less throughout the study,[23] a chronic pattern of stress. These women also exhibited greater depressed moods throughout the day and a harder time transitioning between work and home. Women who felt their homes were more restorative had more normal peaks of cortisol throughout the day.[24] Men didn't have similar results, which suggested that women may be more sensitive to stressful home conditions.

The stress related to clutter doesn't end at our homes. A *Huffington Post* survey found that being stressed about our homes makes us twice as likely to be stressed in general: "Seventy percent of those who were very or extremely stressed about home organization were stressed *in general* every day or almost every day in the past month, versus only thirty-five percent of those who were not worried about home clutter."[25]

When therapy clients experience grief, depression, anxiety, and/or overwhelm, their homes may contribute to those mental conditions. The overwhelming intrusion of stress stems from many areas of life: finances, family responsibilities, work, and hectic schedules. Instead of being a place of relaxation and reprieve, a cluttered home is an additional source of tension. As Susan Krauss Whitbourne states in her article "5 Reasons to Clear the Clutter out of Your Life":

> Living in clutter impedes your identification with your home, which should be a retreat from the outside world and a place to feel pride . . . Having too many of your things in too small a place will lead you to feel that your home environment is your enemy, not your friend.[26]

Home is the one place people can control, and that place should be an escape from life's stressors. Professional organizers can help reduce these stressors by teaching clients to reduce clutter, create systems, and improve efficiency.

Instead of being a place of relaxation and reprieve, a cluttered home is an additional source of tension.

POSSESSIONS AND SELF/ATTACHMENT

Removing clutter helps reduce stress, strengthens the psychological home, and improves subjective well-being. But removing clutter isn't always easy. The purpose of stuff goes well beyond what is useful and functional. Homes and possessions are a reflection of the self. As Dr. Roster says, "Possessions represent not only who we are today, but also who we once were and who we might become in the future . . . Possessions embody the story of our lives and enable us to achieve future goals and aspirations."[27]

People like to own, decorate with, and showcase things that embody their interests, values, accomplishments, and lives. It is important for clients to ask themselves, *What does my home say about me and to me?*

The reason someone holds on to something can be divided into two classes: attachment-seeking or autonomy-seeking. Another way to think of this is whether, through a possession, the client seeks a sense of togetherness (attachment) or individuality (autonomy).

Attachment-Seeking

Meredith beamed with pride as she told me about her mom, Florence, who died a few years earlier. Meredith closed out her mom's estate, but as an only child, most of Florence's possessions came to Meredith's home. In the midst of grieving, it was easier to box things up to deal with later. Later came when she realized that three to four rooms of her home were filled with these boxes, unopened and daunting.

"Mom was an amazing artist. That's most of what I have here," Meredith told me as we looked at one of the rooms filled with boxes of her mom's stuff. Meredith showed me countless pieces created across many artistic mediums: drawings and sketches, beautiful oil paintings on canvas, and sculptures. She flipped through several framed drawings and stopped on one, an ink silhouette of a man and a woman. "This was from our living room. My mom *made* this," Meredith said with emphasis. "She worked on this for weeks and was so proud of it."

Meredith opened the closet door in another room and said, "This closet is all her clothes. I donated the regular stuff already, but this is all things she made herself." The closet was full of brightly-colored, culturally inspired outfits that Florence had carefully crafted. Meredith reached in and touched the sleeve of one dress. "I remember her looking for this fabric. She looked everywhere until she found exactly what she wanted. I was probably seven or eight and she dragged me to so many shops and stores. I remember being so bored! It was worth it though. Look how beautiful this is," Meredith said with a nostalgic smile.

For work, Florence was an influential and respected art teacher at the local high school in her community. "My mom taught those kids everything she could. They learned about artists and methods and materials. They would put on this art show every year to show off all they learned and created. It was the highlight of the year for Mom." In another room, Meredith had more boxes and bins of her mom's teaching supplies. Not just papers and books, but all different paints, fabrics, brushes, patterns, canvases, and sample pieces for every lesson she taught. And perhaps the most difficult to decide about were the pieces of work and notes of gratitude Florence had received from her students.

"I know I can't keep all of this. I need my house back." Meredith sighed. "But I've already done the easy stuff. This . . . " Meredith said as she looked around, ". . . it feels like her. How do I decide about that? Getting rid of something here feels like getting rid of a piece of her." One of Meredith's biggest fears about letting go of her mom's things was that since Meredith herself didn't have kids, these important pieces of her past would just be gone forever.

Meredith's example shows attachment-seeking possessions. Attachment-seeking possessions create a link to family, traditions, and the past. It is the sense of oneness or togetherness that gives these items value. Dr. Roster explains this as, "Attachment-seeking motives align with an individual's need to retain possessions because they represent important connections with others, one's heritage or tradition, or memories that make one feel connected to and cared for by others."[28]

When clients consider parting with these items, there is a fear that, because it represents a memory, relationship, or experience, discarding it would negate the value of that memory, relationship, or experience. Clients feel that without the physical item, the meaning and connection to the past will be severed and lost.[29] And the longer these items are kept, the harder it is to part with them because the objects tend to gain subjective value the longer they are owned.[30]

Autonomy-Seeking

Autonomy-seeking possessions, however, link the client to what makes him/her different. Roster says, "Autonomy-seeking motives align with an individual's need to retain possessions because they represent independence, uniqueness, individual accomplishments."[31] It is because they give the client a sense of individuality that these items have value.

While Meredith's attachment to her mom's things was because of affiliation, Anne's was because of autonomy. Anne was an older woman who had a full career in the corporate world. Retired, she kept herself busy by taking classes at the local college and acting as a substitute teacher at local elementary schools. Her world centered around learning. Anne's biggest challenge was her books. The fourteen bookcases in her small house were beyond full. Even still, there were piles of books everywhere: on her nightstand, next to her living room chair, by the front door, and on the dining room table.

The books' topics were almost as numerous as the books themselves. Anne had books on history, religion, science, literature, business, how-to, self-help, reference, health and beauty, and cookbooks. To Anne, books were not only a pastime, but a passion. She often spoke of why she had certain books, whether it was to prepare for a trip or learn a new skill. She told me stories about why she was interested in a particular topic at one time—stories that often involved some fascinating adventure or personal achievement. The books weren't tying Anne to the past. They were her identity. To Anne, these books represented all that she was, all that she had seen, and all that she accomplished. They symbolized her experience, achievements, and individuality. To discard a book felt like discarding a piece of herself.

When you understand the attachment that clients have to their possessions, whether attachment- or autonomy-seeking, it allows for better understanding of the struggle they have with letting go.

CONTROL AND RESOURCE DEPLETION

A sense of control is a critical part of human happiness. In general, people like to make decisions about their own lives because doing so induces feelings of empowerment, security, and independence. In many aspects of life, such as work or relationships, control may be rendered to or shared with others, but the home is in one's personal domain. The home is a place of personal reflection. It is energizing when the home is an accurate representation of oneself and one that makes its inhabitants feel good (a key part of the psychological home). However, in cluttered and disorganized spaces, the home isn't a place of security, escape, and peace. And living in that type of environment is mentally exhausting.

> *. . . in cluttered and disorganized spaces, the home isn't a place of security, escape, and peace. And living in that type of environment is mentally exhausting.*

An interesting part of loss of control, whether substantiated or perceived, is its effect on mental resources—the ability to focus, make decisions, and prioritize. Lack of control leads to resource depletion. In their article "Environmental Disorder Leads to Self-Regulatory Failure," Boyoun and Rui note:

> According to the limited-resource theory model, people have limited cognitive resources to engage in self-regulation . . . A number of variables have been shown to cause resource depletion, including engaging in cognitively demanding tasks such as suppressing certain thoughts, regulating emotions, overriding automatic responses, engaging in complex tasks, making choices, and changing mind-sets.[32]

Many of these tasks are common in organizing sessions. Organizers encourage clients to create new habits (overriding automatic responses), address overwhelming amounts of clutter (engage in complex tasks), make decisions about possessions (making choices), and change their perceptions about their space and their ability to achieve their organizing goals (changing mind-sets).

After helping Sue and Alan with their garage and estate sale, Sue called me back to work on the clothes in her master bedroom.

The doublewide reach-in closet and two dressers were very full. There were many clothes that did not fit in these spaces and took up residence on the armchair in the corner, bins under the bed, and in piles on the floor. Professional organizer Lissanne Oliver loving refers to this as the "floordrobe."[33] At the start of our session, Sue was highly motivated and quick to make decisions.

Since we worked together before, Sue knew our process to sort items into categories before making decisions about them. Sue was so motivated that she made blanket decisions to speed up our work. "Anything smaller than a size twelve can be donated!" she declared. And, "I'm not fixing any buttons. Anything that needs to be repaired can go!"

It's customary for me to check on my clients' needs throughout a session: "How are you feeling?" "Do you need to stop for a snack?" "Need a five-minute mental break?" Sue didn't want to stop and worked at top-notch speed for about two straight hours. At that point, I held up a pair of pants to ask Sue a question. "Sue, these are labeled size twelve, but they seem larger. Do you want to keep or donate them?"

It took a few seconds for Sue to respond. "I'm not sure. Let me see them," she said, holding out her hand for me to pass them to her. "Oh, I can't remember how these fit. What brand are they? I think they might run large." It's common for clients to stumble on some pieces. Sometimes the pants just need to be tried on. As our session continued, Sue did this for more and more items. "I just don't know," "These are a 'maybe,'" "I'll come back to them later," she would respond.

"Sue, how about a short break? Clear your head a little. I can organize some of the 'keeps' back into the closet while you take a few minutes," I said. I noticed Sue's pace slowing over the past half hour and she was starting to struggle. She showed frustration with herself and with me despite my efforts to match her slowing pace.

"I don't know why we started with the closet. The rest of the room still looks like such a mess," she said, curt and frustrated.

"We started in the closet so that we'll have room to put things that are now out in other places in the room," I replied calmly, to remind Sue of our overall plan.

"Ugh," Sue blurted out, disgusted. "This is never going to get done," she said, her voice rising. "I can't do anymore." She flopped onto the bed.

Sue's comment surprised me. She was usually so optimistic and motivated. I realized the toll the day's work had taken on her. The physical work was demanding, but the mental work was just as hard. Each piece of clothing was a decision Sue had to make. By the end of the day, her brain was tired!

Everyone has limited stores of mental energy. Over time, mentally taxing tasks become more difficult and we become less effective, efficient, and accurate doing them. One result of resource depletion is self-regulatory failure. As one becomes mentally drained, it becomes harder to self-regulate to get motivated, set boundaries, and see a task through to the end. Sue's slowed pace and comments about our progress weren't a reflection of the work we did that day. They were the result of her being mentally tired.

> ### Simply being exposed to disorder is exhausting.

Research suggests that it is not just when people attempt to make changes in their environment that resource depletion is a challenge. Boyoun and Rui state, "Mere exposure to a disorganized environment can lead to resource depletion."[34] Simply being exposed to disorder is exhausting. Boyoun and Rui go on to argue, "a disorganized environment threatens the individual's sense of personal control, and this experience of control threat depletes resources, thus leading to subsequent self-regulatory failure."[35] Disorganization creates an atmosphere of lack of control and ultimately leads to resource depletion and self-regulation failure. This ultimately leads to more disorganized spaces to restart the cycle.

Cycle of Mental Fatigue and Disorganization

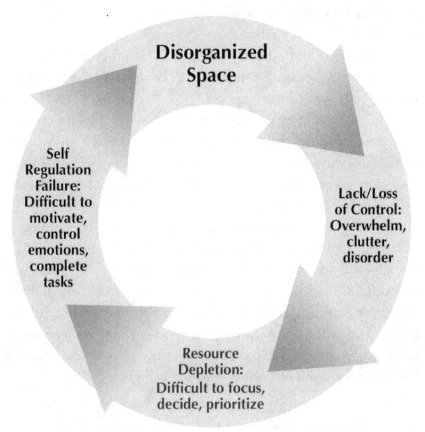

Disorganized Space

Lack/Loss of Control: Overwhelm, clutter, disorder

Resource Depletion: Difficult to focus, decide, prioritize

Self Regulation Failure: Difficult to motivate, control emotions, complete tasks

For professional organizing clients, when their surroundings are in disorder, that environment makes them feel like they don't have control. This lack of control consumes mental energy and depletes defenses such as self-control, motivation, etc. "Belk et al. found that although people who live in a messy environment want a simpler and more organized environment, they usually question their ability to change their environment and perceive their lives as being out of control in general."[36] This is enlightening for professional organizers. Because these clients' resources are already depleted simply by being in their disorganized homes, it is understandable that it is difficult for them to find motivation or stamina to make changes in the space, which creates a more disorganized environment, compounding the effects.

As clients gain order and control in their physical spaces, the subsequent feelings of control can parlay into other parts of their lives.

This connection between disorder, control, and resource deple-tion offers opportunities for both professional organizers and men-tal health professionals. Professional organizers can guide clients to bring control into their physical environment, while mental health professionals can work on the feelings of lack of control in general. As clients gain order and control in their physical spaces, the sub-sequent feelings of control can parlay into other parts of their lives.

PART 3

What Can Be Done?

"Anyone can be taught to increase his/her level of organization. It is never hopeless."[37]
— DIANE HATCHER

CHAPTER 7

Clutter and Related Stress

EIGHTEEN PERCENT OF AMERICANS currently receive mental health services.[38] Comparatively, a staggering amount of people are affected by clutter. A 2017 study done by the *Huffington Post* found that eighty-four percent of Americans worry that their homes aren't organized enough. Given this large percentage, some, if not most, therapy clients experience clutter at home and the related stresses it causes.

If therapists, social workers, psychologists, coaches, and clinicians appreciate this connection of how the physical space and mental state interrelate, it can be used to combine the two aspects of well-being—therapy and organizing—to create a holistic practice that incorporates improving mental health and physical space. In this strategy, you identify and address the emotional elements of a client's life while a professional organizer focuses on the physical space. This is similar to a multi-faceted approach, such as when a personal trainer and nutritionist work together to achieve physical health.

Understanding more about physical space gives you a more complete grasp of your clients' lives and needs—physically, emotionally, and mentally. Clients should be encouraged to work on their physical space as an additional component to therapy and try a strategy that focuses on the mental and physical together. This approach gives clients more immediate and tangible benefits and also improves the results of mental health work. Incorporate learning about clients' homes into assessments of new clients and/or utilize it as a strategy with existing patients for common issues such as depression, grief, and/or anxiety. This may also be helpful in situations where therapy progress has stalled or regressed. It gives you a new avenue to explore with clients and also gives the client something novel and tangible to work on.

> *Understanding more about physical space gives you a more complete grasp of your clients' lives and needs—physically, emotionally, and mentally.*

An added benefit of this approach is that the skills learned in therapy can be transferred to the tasks of organizing and give clients additional opportunities to practice them. Often, the mental health strategies clients learn in therapy are useful in organizing sessions as well. This can be checking in on breathing, practicing reframing, and identifying positive or negative self-talk. For example, as a client complains that there are still so many clothes in their closet after working to purge, organizers may encourage the client to pause, take a few breaths, and re-center. The organizer may review how many bags were designated as donations to reinforce to the client the progress already made. Then the conversation can change from, "There's still so much to do," to, "You've dedicated this time to this and are making progress."

Conversely, bringing the experience of a client's home into therapy sessions also gives concrete examples and opportunities to discuss how therapy's strategies can be applied in a client's everyday life. In discussions about a client's home, they may speak about how the home causes stress. This allows you to teach clients how to readily apply the tools they learn in therapy. They will be back in their homes regularly and repeatedly between sessions—perfect grounds to practice techniques between sessions.

Professional organizers cannot address the stuff without consideration for the emotional elements as well. Therapy cannot address the feelings without consideration of the stuff since they are so deeply connected. Therapy and organizing can each be an asset to the other. As one improves, naturally, so does the other. Both sides are strengthened when the mutual client is supported in both their physical and mental spaces.

The next section covers the steps you can take to incorporate your clients' physical spaces in your therapy approach. This includes learning about the space, introducing the joint approach, and addressing their underlying emotions.

Incorporate Physical Spaces

Learn about client's space → Introduce Collaborative Approach → Address underlying emotions

CHAPTER 8

What Clients Don't Tell You: Their Physical Space

I F YOU AGREE TO LEARN MORE about your clients' physical spaces, your first reaction might be, *I see clients in my office. How can I know what their homes look like?* Great question! There are ways to learn how a client's home looks and feels—questions and visual tools, and assessments.

Questions to Ask

I often remind my children, if you don't know something, ask. This applies to learning about client spaces as well. In my initial phone calls with prospective clients, I need to learn more about their homes. So, I ask, "Tell me about your home. Do you rent or own?" "Who lives with you?" "What do you think is the most challenging room in your home?" "If we could bring order to just one space in your home, which one would you like it to be?" These questions are not about the stuff! It is about the space and the feelings associated with those spaces. While tackling their stuff is a means, the end goal is to improve how clients *feel* in their space.

In talk therapy, it's helpful to know what questions to ask clients to learn about their physical spaces. The questions on the next page can help start the living space conversation:

- What is the first thing you notice when you walk into your home?
- What is your favorite room? Why do you like it?
- What is your least favorite room? Why don't you like it?
- Do you park in your garage? Sleep in your bed? Why or why not?
- What do you do with the mail when you bring it in?
- Do you feel that your home is an escape from life's stressors?
- How do the others who live with you feel about your home?

These questions have a dual purpose. First, they allow you to learn more about your client's physical space with the goal to find the visceral, underlying emotion.

Once, on an initial intake phone call, I asked a prospective client which room was her favorite. She said it was her bathroom! This was the first time I ever heard this answer so I was curious to find out why. She said, "It's the only room that doesn't have stuff everywhere. It's so peaceful in there." Ah! It wasn't due to amenities or function. The bathroom was an escape to her!

Second, these questions make a client aware of how their physical space makes them feel. Since all of my clients contact me *because* of their physical space, they are aware that it causes them some sort of distress. However, therapy clients may not consider this connection between their homes and their feelings. The answers to these questions might bring to light some of the tensions, challenges, and feelings that are mirrored in their (physical) home life, and this offers the mental health provider a segue to explain the connection between the physical and mental spaces.

> . . . these questions make a client aware of how their physical space makes them feel.

Photos/Videos of Space

If they're comfortable doing it, clients can take pictures or videos of their home to share with you. Like the questions above, these pictures have a dual purpose too. Yes, it will be helpful to see what a client's home looks like. But taking pictures and looking at the space from a third-party perspective can be enlightening for the client as well. Oftentimes, clutter becomes less apparent when it's seen every day. Because clients are not looking for the clutter, it simply becomes part of their homes' norm and landscape. I call this "inattentional blindness." When I work with clients one-on-one, I call their attention to clutter they no longer even notice. It may simply be asking, "Why does the laundry pile here?" or, "Tell me about the papers that collect on the counter." Seeing their homes through photos or video can call their attention to that which they normally overlook. And these realizations can become the basis for conversations with both their professional organizer and/or therapist.

SITUATIONAL VS. CHRONIC DISORGANIZATION

Clutter creates two types of disorganization. In the professional organizing world, disorganization is categorized as either situational or chronic.[40][41] The mental health challenges associated with each type of clutter is addressed differently. In situational disorganization, the person may experience grief or a difficult time of transition. In chronic disorganization, there may be other issues such as ADHD or past trauma.

Situational Disorganization

In situational disorganization, clutter or chaos is experienced for a short period of time and is usually a result of some life event or change in living arrangements. This can be the birth of a child, the joining of two homes, a move, a new job, a new disability, or any change in routine.

Helen wrote to me because she felt frustrated by her family home. She had several spots in her home and life that she wanted to declutter and reorganize to make them more functional. She identified herself as a "self-starter," and knew that if we even just created an action plan, she would be able to execute it. She told me all this in her introduction email before we even spoke on the phone!

Helen was in her sixties, retired, and raised two now-grown children. At our in-person assessment, I was impressed with her clear goals and focus. She said, "I want to be able to read the paper at the table on Sunday and know exactly what I have coming up for the week. I want to be able to have people over without worrying about cleaning up or putting things away. And I want a plan for how I keep it that way!"

Helen's biggest frustration was that her hobbies and travel took over her space and her schedule. She explained, "Things get started, but not finished so they get left out. I mean, I might work on a scrapbook project and I don't want to put it all away in the middle of it. But then I get so busy that I don't ever have time to work on it, so it sits out forever."

Hobby projects like this were a challenge for Helen and she had lots of them: knitting, scrapbooking, journaling, painting, and home projects. Added to this were tasks like travel planning, packing, and the dreaded unpacking. Her days were definitely busy, but they didn't feel productive to her.

"I used to accomplish so much in a day, now I feel so busy but feel like nothing ever gets done," Helen said to me.

"When did that change for you?" I asked.

"Oh, a few years now. Probably since the kids have grown up," she said. "I don't know how I did it when they were younger. I was so on top of things! We were so busy then, but I guess the house had different clutter then too. I remember it feeling chaotic at times, but not like this. This just feels like everything is everywhere all the time."

Helen experienced situational disorganization. Her life circumstances changed, and with that, many of the foundations of her organization systems were gone too. She did well with the routines of school days and structured weeks. Ever since her children moved out, Helen began to feel disorganized. Her many hobbies took over her time and space. Days could slip away unproductive since Helen simply didn't know where to focus.

I worked with Helen to identify her new hobbies, what supplies she needed for each, and where each hobby was done. To create some physical order, we reorganized some spaces based on which hobby was done there. Painting was done in the basement near her painting supplies. We set up an area for knitting and scrapbooking in a spare bedroom. Journaling was done whenever or wherever the mood struck her, so we created a portable system that could hold and transport her supplies to wherever she needed them.

We also worked to structure Helen's day. Helen knew she was unlikely to plan her activities too far in advance. Instead, we worked on a morning routine that allowed her to review her calendar to see if any important events were coming up that she wanted to prepare for and also let her see how much free time she had available in the day for her hobbies. We added a running to-do list on a white board in her kitchen so she could easily see her current projects. This allowed her to keep them top of mind and prioritize them. A few simple routines helped Helen regain the structure she thrived on when her kids were younger.

When people experience situational disorganization, it may influence and/or exacerbate their feelings of overwhelm, anxiety, pressure, etc. It can be unsettling for them to suddenly feel that they don't have control in this area of their lives. In situational disorganization, we can usually identify some key components of the client's life that create the disorganization and restore a sense of order, which eases the mental health drains that disorganization can cause.

Chronic Disorganization

Chronic disorganization is more complicated because it is a long-standing and ongoing state. Chronic disorganization clients recall being disorganized in the past, perhaps for many years, and often back to childhood. The state of disorder significantly impacts their daily life. Many with chronic disorganization make self-help attempts, but efforts are not sustainable. This often leads to feelings of discouragement and the expectation that they will be disorganized in the future.[42] Imagine the emotions that come along with this cycle of thinking!

Chronic disorganization is addressed differently than situational disorganization. Chronic disorganization clients make more gradual changes and build on existing routines.

From our first conversation I heard the despair in Michelle's voice as she told me about her home—"I have some moving boxes that I haven't unpacked, and I just feel like I can't do them on my own. They've been sitting in my dining room for months." At first, I thought this was situational disorganization, that the transition of the move prompted disorder in her home. As we talked more about what she was experiencing, I realized that chronic disorganization was more likely.

"It's always been like this," Michelle told me on that first phone call. "Even when I was a kid my mom would get so frustrated with my room being a mess that she would clean it up herself." When her mom stepped in, Michelle never had to learn the skills to get organized. She struggled in school because papers would get lost or she would forget to study for tests. It became worse as Michelle got older. The moving boxes were just a symptom of her overall challenge. Incoming mail, bill paying, being on time, home maintenance, being able to think about anything beyond right now . . . she struggled with all of these. She lamented, "I'm always trying, but it never sticks. I've read all the books and set things up the way they say to and it looks great . . . for a little while. It's everywhere, every room, and it never ends."

Large, broad strategies like I set up with Helen wouldn't work with Michelle. Her experience of her space was different. Michelle couldn't picture herself being organized because she didn't know what that looked like for herself. She needed help to figure out that big picture, but also needed small, guided steps to get there.

My approach with Michelle was granular. We worked on one space at a time and built routines one step at a time. The goal was to create one step of a routine that aided Michelle's organization skills. Once Michelle practiced and mastered that step, we added another to the routine. For those moving boxes that prompted Michelle's first call, we sorted them, unopened, into piles for each room. Then together we practiced unpacking one box at a time, start to finish, decided where things should go, and followed through on those decisions by actually moving the items. As we practiced this routine over the first few boxes, Michelle gained confidence in her ability to do it herself as she mastered the routine.

Of course, the chronic-ness of chronic disorganization meant that Michelle needed help in many areas of her home and life beyond those boxes. Whereas with Helen we set up the systems and she felt that the change was complete, Michelle needed more accountability and support to make her changes successful. We worked on several areas in her home over a few months and set up a call once a month to provide Michelle accountability and support. I checked in to see how the routines we set up worked and if any adjustments were needed. Those calls kept Michelle on track and allowed her to set goals for the upcoming month. She was no longer stuck in the "right now" of her disorganization. She could move forward in her life with more clarity and purpose.

It is easy to understand how feeling disorganized your whole life can result in feelings of depression, anxiety, and disappointment. Managing chronic disorganization empowers clients. It offers hope that they can accomplish their goals and be successful in their efforts in the future.

Understanding whether a therapy client experiences situational or chronic disorganization will be helpful. Each has different causes and different mental health aspects related to it. Both Helen and Michelle's disorganization caused them mental distress. Therapy clients may experience similar feelings: confusion, depression, overwhelm, or defeat. If you understand the type of disorganization your client has, expectations can be set about the impact it has on their lives and the efforts needed to address it.

CLUTTER QUALITY OF LIFE SCALE (CQLS)

Once what a client's home looks like (questions and photos/videos) and the type of clutter (situational or chronic) has been established, it is crucial to know *how* that clutter affects the client. It is imperative to find out if the client finds the clutter bothersome or if it has consequences that affect their quality of life.

> . . . it is crucial to know how that clutter affects the client.

The Clutter Quality of Life Scale (CQLS) shows how clutter affects the quality of life for an individual. This scale was developed by academic and author Catherine Roster of the University of New Mexico in collaboration with the Institute for Challenging Disorganization (ICD). It:

> is designed to measure inward, or subjective, consequences of clutter from the individual's perspective. As such, it provides an indirect assessment of a person's well-being by measuring personally felt negative consequences of clutter in that person's life across important life domains commonly associated with quality of life.[43]

The scale assesses a client's satisfaction with clutter levels and their physical space through multiple questions in four key areas:

- Livability of Space: How rooms function, access to items and spaces, and safety
  - Example: I can't find things when I need them because of clutter.
- Emotional: Depression, guilt, and worry
  - Example: I feel guilty when I think about the clutter in my home.
- Social: Interpersonal conflict and interactions.
  - Example: My family life has suffered as a result of the clutter in my home.

- Financial: Debt and monetary consequences
  - Example: I often buy things I already have because I don't know where things are in my home.

The scale is available electronically and scored online. (A paper version is also available.) Clients rate each of the eighteen statements on a scale of 1 to 7. A composite score combines all four areas and provides insight into how clutter affects a client. A lower score indicates that clutter has a lower impact on the person's subjective quality of life. A higher score indicates a higher impact. The CQLS tool is particularly useful because it gives a quantitative measure to a client's subjective experience of their space.

While these tools are a starting point for conversations with clients, they can also be used throughout the therapy process. The questions can be revisited, and updated photos taken to see the progress made or start a conversation about ongoing challenges.

Once a mental health professional has a clear appreciation of their client's physical home life and if/how they are affected by clutter, the next step is to introduce the collaborative approach to work on the mental and physical spaces simultaneously.

CHAPTER 9

Introduce a Collaborative Approach

OW CAN YOU MOVE FROM, "This is how it is," and "This is how it feels for my clients," to "This is what we do"? First, expect that clients are not aware of this connection, and propose it as a possible new approach to consider. Next, introduce them to the work of professional organizers as a resource to help improve both their physical and mental spaces.

INTRODUCE THE CONNECTION TO CLIENTS

Imagine trying to get into better physical shape. Perhaps you want to lose weight, have your clothes fit better, or add a few pounds of muscle. To achieve these changes, you hit the gym five times a week. You add in cardio and weight lifting. After a few weeks you start to see some small changes, not only with how you look, but also how you feel. That flight of stairs doesn't steal your breath anymore. That pair of pants slips on a little easier.

Even though you are consistent and committed to the gym, you haven't made similar positive changes in your diet. You still grab convenience foods. Late night snacking is a common habit. More calories go in than get used.

We all know the basic science of weight loss. Diet and exercise both need to be part of the plan to create a well-rounded system.

Let's say you improve your diet, bring in healthy fats, cut out processed foods, and increase veggies. If you do your thing in the gym and make these changes to your diet, the results skyrocket. Doing either is fine, but doing them together creates real change. It becomes less about working out or dieting, and more about strategy and lifestyle.

The same is true of mental health and physical space work. They are complementary. Working on both simultaneously is about overall life improvement. It's not about the stuff, the space, or the feelings independently. It's about how each relates to the others and how all three need to be part of the solution. This is a great starting point for discussions with clients about making changes in their homes to promote better mental health.

Understanding the physical look of a client's space through questions and photos is just the first part. It is also crucial for both you and your client to understand their personal experience with clutter and how it influences them, such as measured by the CQLS. Talking through their responses about their space and stuff allows the client to qualify, perhaps for the first time, how their external environment influences them internally. This is also why most of the introductory questions focus on the feelings a space evokes as opposed to just about the stuff. The client's experience of clutter and the influence it has on their lives is just a symptom of the underlying feelings associated with clutter. Bringing clients' attention to this influence is one of the first steps to help them see the issue, accept its influence, and initiate change.

> The client's experience of clutter and the influence
> it has on their lives is just a symptom of the underlying
> feelings associated with clutter.

Subjectivity of Clutter and Organization

Most of my clients want to know if their home is the worst I've ever seen, or they wonder why I ask so many questions about things other than the stuff. I think they worry that I have either some preconceived notion about their home or am waiting to ambush them with a grand reveal about why their home is disorganized. Neither is true.

Each individual has its own threshold for when a space is disorganized because clutter and disorganization are subjective. For clutter to be a problem, it needs to be just that, a problem. It is important for you to discuss the subjectivity of clutter and disorganization because it erases the expectation of a "one size fits all" or "perfect" solution. Understanding and allowing for this subjectivity empowers clients because it creates an atmosphere of control. Control is a key factor in the psychological home and subjective well-being. The client controls what is considered clutter in their homes. They control what level of "neatness" constitutes organization.

Ask clients what *does* work in their homes. These are things that should not change. If something works for that household, then it falls within the subjective definition of organized. This question helps clients understand that the process of getting organized revolves around their own family's needs and that they do, in fact, have the ability to be organized.

ENGAGE A PROFESSIONAL ORGANIZER

Once invested in the connection between their homes and their mental well-being, some clients may decide to make changes in their homes on their own. Others may need more guidance, accountability, and support. For the latter, a professional organizer can be an incredible resource.

Making clients aware that these services exist makes them more attainable. Some clients may not be aware of the services available and others may only associate professional organizing work with extreme cases. When I say I am a professional organizer, I still hear, "Like on *Hoarders*?" about twenty percent of the time. My response is always, "No, like you're overwhelmed by your mail being a daily burden or your garage is full of stuff and you'd rather it not be. I help with that." Everyone can relate to those examples: everyday people, everyday stuff.

Clients may not be sure what to expect from working with an organizer or how to find one who is a good fit. Understanding the work of organizers allows you to discuss such uncertainties. A key point is to know that each organizer has his or her own approach, philosophies, and areas of expertise. It benefits clients to reach out to several organizers to see who is the best fit for them personally. Clients should feel comfortable being open and honest with the organizer and know that the organizer works in the client's best interests.

Likeness of Professional Organizing to Therapy

Organizing and therapy work similarly on many planes: time, intimacy, confidentiality, variability, and uniqueness. You can show clients the similarities between the two as a way to assuage fears or uncertainty about including organizing in their therapy work. It also sets the expectation that the organizing process will be unique to them and will take time and commitment to achieve the greatest results.

CONNECT WITH POS

Even if clients are aware that organizing services exist, it may be hard to know where to find someone reputable. Having connections with local organizers is advantageous because a personal referral from a trusted source is very valuable to clients.

I am grateful when my clients share their organizing experience with their friends, family, and colleagues. First, it normalizes the service. A prospective client may think, *Susie is similar to me and she needed help with this too. It's okay to need help with this.* Second, people who struggle with clutter and disorganization may be hesitant to seek out referrals from others. Either they do not know that such services exist or they may not realize that the majority of organizing clients are everyday people! It can be embarrassing or uncomfortable to say to someone else, "I need help with this private, even secretive, part of my life that I normally hide from others. Can you recommend someone?" Not only does it create vulnerability for the person asking, but it also implies that the person they are seeking advice from has needed that help in the past. Having organizer referrals at the ready can help clients avoid this apprehension and embarrassment.

It is important to note that the threshold to start an organizing career is very low, unlike the mental health field where schooling, training, and supervised practice are required. Look for legitimate professional organizers who have registered business entities, are members of professional associations such as NAPO and ICD, and who obtain training through specialist certificates and the CPO® (Certified Professional Organizer®) and CPO-CD® (Certified Professional Organizer in Chronic Disorganization®) certifications. Such professional organizers have committed themselves to professionalism, education, and adherence to ethics.

To find a local qualified professional organizer, the first stop can be the National Association of Productivity and Organizing Professionals (NAPO). NAPO is the professional association of the industry. NAPO's mission is to "be the leading source for Organizing and Productivity Professionals by providing exceptional education, enhancing business connections, advancing industry research, and increasing public awareness."[44] NAPO's professional members take foundation classes on professional organizing, adhere to a code of ethics, have access to education on numerous organizing topics, and are part of a supportive community that shares ideas and resources.

NAPO has several chapters throughout the country, which hold regular meetings for members and guests. Attending a local chapter meeting is a great way to meet several professional organizers and learn more about how NAPO educates its members.

Another resource is the Institute for Challenging Disorganization (ICD). ICD members are generally professional organizers who specialize in chronic disorganization. Their expertise focuses on hoarding disorder, ADHD, and other neurological disorders that influence productivity and organization. Although there aren't ICD chapters throughout the country, ICD has a search feature to find qualified organizers based on location, specialty, or certification.

When to Introduce

The choice of when to introduce this connection to a client depends on your individual practices, relationship with the client, and the client themselves. This connection can be a delicate, overwhelming, and extremely personal one. You may choose to not introduce it when you feel other aspects of the client's mental health take precedence, or if the client is being seen for reasons unrelated to their possessions. Conversely, this connection may be introduced very early on with clients who struggle with grief, anxiety, or depression and who could benefit from gaining control over their physical space. This concept is meant to create an additional therapeutic tool if/when it fits with your client's needs.

CHAPTER 10

Addressing Underlying Emotions

AS A MENTAL HEALTH PROFESSIONAL, you fulfill your role in this collaborative approach in two ways. The first is to address the emotions that result from physical spaces and that physical spaces cause such as overwhelm, fear, grief, sentimentality, etc. Next is to provide clients with additional tools to aid in their success—setting goals, developing realistic expectations, and providing accountability.

The organizing process is emotional for clients, but it is outside the expertise and qualifications of professional organizers to help clients through these emotions. This is where professional organizers need you as their partners. You are trained to work with clients to embrace, utilize, and transform their feelings that surround their clutter. This usually presents the opportunity to find and tear down the emotional roadblocks that hinder the client's progress in both therapy and with their clutter. As Ryan Howes writes in his Psychology Today article, "A therapist's role is to encourage clients to directly face reality so they can take control and live their best possible life; only by being truthful with themselves and others can clients identify their biggest obstacles and progress toward their goals."[45] Considering both physical space and mental state allows your clients to have a more truthful understanding of their lives and aids them in reaching their goals.

> *This usually presents the opportunity to find and tear down the emotional roadblocks that hinder the client's progress in both therapy and with their clutter.*

The Toxic Five: Embarrassment, Shame, Guilt, Fear of Failure, Vulnerability.

Many clients have a range of emotions linked not only to their items in particular, but to the overall state of their homes. These feelings include embarrassment, shame, guilt, fear of failure, and vulnerability. It is extremely common for new clients to ask, "Is this the worst you've ever seen?" or, "How 'should' it look?" Negative, overarching feelings about their space in general are common. Consider how clients are bombarded with "Insta-worthy" and "Pinterest Perfect" ideas of how homes should look and function and what societal pressures they experience from friends, family and culture.

Also consider how the physical look of a home is just one component of these pressures. It is in addition to how successful someone "should" be, what trips one "should" take, and what activities kids "should" do. These are all examples of high-pressure culture with unattainable standards of living, and these all influence quality of life.

These emotions expose internal or external pressures that the client may feel regarding their space. Talking through these pressures can help you and your clients understand both the personal and societal expectations they perceive, and later decide whether to accept or reject these expectations.

Client Hesitation

Expect that some clients may be hesitant to share information about their physical home space. They may feel that it's irrelevant, embarrassing, or overwhelming. To ease into the simultaneous approach, perhaps talk first just about the hesitation instead of about the space and stuff. This begins the conversation on the emotional component of physical space before the client has to divulge anything else. It keeps the conversation squarely in the realm of mental health until the client is open to learning about the connection between physical and mental spaces.

Expect that some clients may be hesitant to share information about their physical home space.

I use a similar approach on the organizing side. If I've mentioned the connection to the emotional aspects of organizing but the client seems hesitant to think about them, I suggest that we work only on areas that don't have an intense emotional component so that they can become more familiar with the physical side of organizing first. Often, as they experience change in the physical space, they feel the emotional change as well, and they become more open to applying the connection to our work.

Honesty, Confidentiality, and Non-Judgment

Due to the highly personal and intimate context of both fields, therapists and organizers need to remind clients that they support not judge, help not shame. When clients believe their therapist and organizer are members of their team, it allows them to trust and create the change that they seek. Particularly when a client is hesitant, reiterate a commitment to honesty, confidentiality, and non-judgment to help reinforce the expectation of therapy and organizing as safe spaces.

ADDITIONAL TOOLS

The preference is for clients to work with both a professional organizer and a therapist simultaneously. Even if the client wants to work on both spaces, this may not always be possible due to personal resistance to the idea, finances, or scheduling. If a therapy client decides to work on their own, they may need some suggestions on how to tackle their physical space.

"Where do I start?" is usually a client's first question. Much as your role is to help the client decide where to start in their mental space, organizers help clients decide where to start in their physical space. One suggestion is to start in the space that the client considers the easiest. This may mean that it is the smallest space or the one that has the easiest decisions to make. For example, a pantry may be a good starting point because of its small size and because it's unlikely to stir many deep-rooted feelings. There is likely little emotional attachment to the pantry and its contents. Decisions are easier to make because they are based on expiration dates and common, prefabricated categories such as baking, pasta, and condiments. Something like this as a starting point gives the client practice on the organizing process and teaches them the techniques that will be used on harder areas in the future. It also gives them a sense of control, knowledge, and accomplishment, which are powerful small victories.

Another starting approach is to begin in the space that will have the most impact day-to-day. When a client struggles with where to begin, the master bedroom is a good recommendation. The master bedroom is where days begin and end. The emotional effects of clutter surrounding this location can be defeating. When the client starts in the bedroom, they create a place that is an escape from the other stressors of the home. For other clients, high traffic spots such as the entryway and kitchen may be good starting points. It may be best to bring order and calm to these places first since they are commonly the source of so much tension.

Sometimes, the best starting point may not be a location at all, but instead a type of item. Say, for example, that an abundance of clothes is the stressor. The starting point might be to move five pieces of clothing a day to a donation bag.

It is important to note that very few places or items in homes exist in isolation. Homes work as a unit and there is a fluidity that occurs across spaces and items. Work on the pantry also influences the kitchen. Work on the master bedroom also influences the closets. Work on the clothes involves multiple places in the home where clothes are ultimately stored.

While the client wants to make an informed and sensible choice for where to begin, the most important thing is to simply start.

Set Goals

Goal setting is a way to have an intention at the beginning of a process. The advantage of goal setting is that it allows clients to work toward something. It keeps the end point in sight to ensure they stay on track in the right direction. It also creates a way to measure progress: *I've done this and this, and now I am closer to where I want to be.*

Through goal setting, the client verbalizes what they hope to accomplish through therapy and organizing. The goal can be physical or emotional. A physical goal may be: *My goal is to reduce the number of books of the bookshelf by half within the next two weeks.* Or the goal can be emotional: *My goal is to feel calm and restful in this space at the end of each day.* Having a goal means that the client can make decisions in all their actions: *Does this action/item bring me closer to or farther away from my goal?*

Among others, Pam, the stay-at-home mom with four young children, had one particular goal she wanted to focus on. "I want the boys to be able to clean up after themselves without me having to direct them," she said to me. This was attainable, but not exactly straightforward. We had to flesh out what "clean up" meant to Pam, what obstacles the boys would face, and how they would learn the new skills.

"What areas do you want the boys to be responsible for?" I asked.

"Definitely the playroom to start. It's all their stuff, so they should be able to clean it up," she said confidently.

"When you say, 'clean it up,' what does that mean? How does that look to you?" I asked.

Pam paused a moment and then said, "I know they like to leave some stuff out that they play with every day, like the Legos and trains. I'm okay with that, but everything else, like the action figures and costumes, and whatever this is," she said, holding up what looked like a toy car with swords that protruded from every angle, "should be put away."

"Do the boys know where to put things away?" I asked.

"Yes and no. We have these cubbies and bins and the toy organizer over there," Pam said as she pointed to the other wall. "They know that everything goes into the bins, but when they help me clean up, they mix everything up. They throw everything in whatever bin is closest. They think it if it's off the floor, then they're done. But then next time they want to play with something, they can't find it," she said.

"So, they need some guidance on how to clean up?" I asked as Pam nodded her head. "We'll have to think about how we can teach them."

If the ultimate goal is large or far away, such as Pam's boys being completely independent to clean up the playroom, clients can get discouraged along the way. Smaller goals are more useful. Smaller victories allow clients to celebrate their progress throughout the process, which is just as important.

For Pam, we gradually transferred responsibility for the playroom to the boys. At first, we let the boys help set up the systems in the playroom so that cleaning up would be more intuitive to them. They decided things like all the good guy action figures should be separated from the bad guy action figures and even drew their own colorful, graphic labels for the bins. Next, Pam needed to be there to guide them in how to clean up with the system we created while the boys did the work. Over time, they became more independent until they did it completely on their own.

You can talk to your clients about home goals and encourage them to think about what "done" really looks and, more importantly, feels like. Perhaps they aim for a home that feels peaceful and restful, or one that is structured and ordered. Perhaps they aim to entertain more. Whatever their motivation, clear goals support their desire to create a home that feels good to be in.

Define Realistic Expectations

Sometimes clients have very lofty expectations of what organizing work will be able to accomplish. Yes, the images on the cover of *Real Simple* magazine look beautiful, but is that realistic? How much money and how many hours did it take to get that look? Does anyone actually live in that space? How much effort would it require to keep it like that?

Expectations can relate to a space, a function, or a time. Dimensions limit space. Twenty linear feet of books will not magically fit onto a five-foot shelf. Configuration and use limit function. A ten-by-ten bedroom shared by two kids cannot also hold two desks, reading chairs, and a fully assembled, five-thousand-piece Lego set.

Time is a favorite expectation to share with clients. Amazingly, the time needed to complete a task can be grossly over- or under-estimated. I often ask clients to estimate how long a particular task will take and then time the actual task to show the difference. This can be something simple like the time it takes to fold and put away laundry or clean out a junk drawer. Half of the time clients estimate the task will take much less time than it actually does. This is as an opportunity to encourage clients to start on something that they think will take very long to complete. They might surprise themselves! Have you ever experienced this? You put off something for days, weeks, or even longer. It is a nuisance but you leave it undone anyway. And then when you actually do the task, you are frustrated that you allowed yourself to be inconvenienced for so long since the task was so much simpler to complete than you expected.

I recently did this with a cabinet full of lidded cups that my kids use. I knew they used the same four or five most of the time, but there were at least fifteen in the cabinet. More than once they all toppled out onto the counter when I tried to shimmy one free. I was frustrated every time I went in there, but still made all the regular excuses: "I can't go through them now because I'm in a rush." "Some are in the sink. I need them all clean so I can look at them all at once." Finally, out of frustration, I just grabbed five that I knew hadn't been used in months and tossed them into recycling. Then I took out two more. I reduced the count by half in about thirty seconds. It wasn't perfect, but I no longer feared an avalanche every time I opened the cabinet. And I wondered why I waited so long to do such a simple task. Yes, even I do these things. I'm organized, not perfect.

The opposite time effect also happens when things take much longer to complete than expected. *I'll just get this done. It should only take a few minutes*, you think. But an hour later you are still at work on the same task. Inefficient estimates inhibit time management because it is difficult to schedule tasks and their expected completion time/date if there isn't a realistic expectation about how long something takes to accomplish. Encourage clients to estimate the expected time before a task and then compare it to the actual time when they finish. This helps clients to notice these variances and plan accordingly in the future.

Reigning in expectations is a necessary service to clients. Yes, they should be motivated and think big, but it is better to reign in expectations in the beginning as opposed to letting them spend time, effort, money, and energy on something that may not be probable, if even possible. This helps prevent clients from feeling like a failure when they struggle to meet some impossible standard.

Accountability

The power of accountability cannot be underestimated. Clients who feel accountable and supported in both the mental and physical aspects of their lives have an improved likelihood of success. Each therapy session is an opportunity for the client to give an account of how they did since the last session. This might be something they practiced or a new approach they tried. It means they have to be responsible to someone outside of themselves, which can be a powerful tool for change. I personally told a lot of people about writing this book. I didn't want to embarrass myself by not doing it once I said I was. And I wanted to be able to give them positive updates whenever they asked about it. They kept me accountable.

Both you and professional organizers act as accountability partners for clients. Both set scheduled times to meet. The client has agreed to meet at a certain time for a certain length of time. It is more difficult to cancel plans when someone else is involved. Plenty of my clients would happily avoid organizing if I didn't ring their doorbell at our scheduled time.

Next, both you and professional organizers follow up with clients about what they worked on last time and anything they were expected to do between sessions. This accountability is a reminder to the client of the team approach. Both you and the organizer should ask about these things since they are important tasks to accomplish. The client's role is to do them. To know someone will ask about their progress is motivating. I meet with several of my clients for accountability calls, scheduled check-ins throughout the month to help keep them on task for organizing work or maintenance goals. At each call we review what was done since the last call, set new goals, and schedule our next call. This accountability keeps them focused and moving forward, even if the majority of the work is done just before our call starts. Done is done, right? Accountability is a critical piece of the support system that clients need to succeed.

Both also help keep clients focused on larger goals. Once the client establishes what he or she wants to accomplish, either physically or mentally, the professional relationships keep them accountable to work toward that. Both you and the organizer need to keep those goals at the forefront of the client's mind. This also means reminding clients of *why* they work toward that goal. In the day-to-day work of self-improvement, the why can get lost in the struggle. If a client chooses to work on their organizing goals without the help of a professional organizer you can fulfill the role of their accountability partner.

> *Once the client establishes what he or she wants to accomplish, either physically or mentally, the professional relationships keep them accountable to work toward that. Both the therapist and organizer need to keep those goals at the forefront of the client's mind.*

Maintenance

An additional means of support for clients is to encourage maintenance in their physical space practices. Maintenance restores order in the current situation and prevents large problems from resurfacing. Maintenance keeps the results of organizing work viable. It is the key component that makes organizing a process instead of a project. Small maintenance efforts done consistently keep a space looking and feeling great. It also provides for easy victories, which creates feelings of control, competence, and success.

The initial act of decluttering and organizing feels transformative. However, regression, and all the complicated feelings that surround it, is likely if there isn't a plan in place to maintain the progress. All of my clients are given a plan for maintenance at every session. I ask, "How do we keep this space like this until we meet again?" and we talk through strategies that are realistic for the client to implement and duplicate.

Similar exercises are done in therapy. Not every session is about breakthroughs and moving forward. At some sessions, a client's progress needs to be reassessed to determine if there has been backslide and find ways to re-center. I recall at some of my own therapy sessions we would review my "toolbox" to remind me of breathing and reframing strategies and allow me to reinstitute them. It wasn't anything new, but it was an important reminder that I had these tools and could reach for them when needed.

Change in Clients

Whether a client decides to work with a professional organizer on his or her space or to work independently, the advantages of working on physical and mental spaces simultaneously can be transformative. Just as the body responds best to diet and exercise together, the approach of therapy and organizing together creates a holistic strategy. Because of their connectedness, both spaces influence the other. They don't operate independently. They work in tandem. Changes in one, whether positive or negative, have a ripple effect on the other. To create a change or find clarity in either influences the other. And efforts in one make the other less overwhelming.

> . . . the approach of therapy and organizing together creates a holistic strategy. Because of their connectedness, both spaces influence the other.

Expect changes in clients as they clear their physical spaces. When organizing brings emotions to the surface, those emotions can be addressed to create improved mental space and allow the client the energy and mental clarity to also clear the physical space. In addition to their simplified homes, clients who are also in therapy report greater motivation, more progress in therapy sessions, and experience more lasting change in mental and physical space.

PART 4

Common Feelings

"Out of clutter, find simplicity."
— ALBERT EINSTEIN

CHAPTER 11

The Emotional Connection

M Y WORK AS A PROFESSIONAL ORGANIZER is to help clients reduce clutter and create systems so that their homes and lives can function simply and efficiently. In the simplest sense, this starts with people's stuff. More often than not, clients call me because they feel so overwhelmed not just by the stuff, but by the emotions attached to their things. To deal with the physical stuff they also need accountability, guidance, and support. Clutter isn't just about the stuff—it is about how they *feel* about the stuff.

> *Clutter isn't just about the stuff—it is about how they feel about the stuff.*

A few feelings generally emerge as I work with my clients: sentimentality, fear, indecision, and overwhelm/defeat. Of course, this list is not inclusive of the rainbow of emotions clients feel as we work through their physical space. Clients also show anger, regret, shame, and embarrassment to name a few more. The emotions here are ones that I commonly see and that I have developed strategies for. My goal is to guide my clients through the organizing process while I also acknowledge the emotions they feel about their stuff.

As we begin to discuss the most common feelings, attachments, and emotions, clients often experience multiple reactions. One object, space, or experience can elicit many feelings all at once. For example, John may know that to go through his deceased wife's clothes will be difficult due to his feelings of grief. However, when he opens the closet door and sees the volume of clothes, shoes, and accessories, and the corresponding number of decisions he will have to make, it also feels overwhelming at the same time. Each emotion isn't experienced in a vacuum, and it is common for clients to experience many and/or cycle through different emotions throughout the organizing process or even in a single organizing session.

In therapy sessions, mental health providers can listen for the common phrases clients often say when they speak about their clutter. Such phrases give clues to which emotions clients feel as they go through the organizing process. Within the HIPAA guidelines and with the client's permission, it may also be beneficial for the mental health professional and professional organizer to meet and discuss their mutual client. You will also have insight into other emotions the client experiences since your conversations extend beyond their physical surroundings. You are in a unique position to draw parallels for your client about how feelings they address in therapy may also result in clutter in their physical space.

CHAPTER 12

"That was my mom's."
Feelings of Sentimentality

M ANY CLIENTS WHO EXPERIENCE DIFFICULTY with sentimental things also have feelings of grief, guilt, fear, and overwhelm. It goes far beyond what a person has physically in their
home. Clients can have attachments to objects because they make
them feel connected to the past, traditions, their culture, and important people in their lives.

As I started in my career as a professional organizer, I was aware
that certain objects would have sentimental feelings attached. I was
prepared for this with pieces such as photos or family heirlooms, but
I didn't understand how various objects could be sentimental. As I
became more experienced, I recognized the same types of phrases, "This was my mom's," or, "I remember that from when I was a
kid," with all types of things—jewelry, trophies, greeting cards, notes,
t-shirts, artwork. My husband even had an attachment to a rock from
his mother's home. It was a smooth river stone with the word "wis-
dom" carved into it. The joke in his family was that this was the
"mopsim" rock since that was what the word looked like upside down.

Sentimentality is as subjective as organizing itself. There is no
clear boundary for what qualifies as important and meaningful.
Each client will have different levels of sentimental attachment to

any number of things. Awareness of this subjectivity means talking to clients to learn what kinds of items evoke feelings of sentimentality for them and why.

> *Sentimentality is as subjective as organizing itself.*

HOW TO IDENTIFY SENTIMENTALITY

So often sentimental items are left for years, if not generations, untouched. These items can be very difficult for clients because they feel torn between the physical object and the feelings it elicits, whether positive, such as love and nostalgia, or negative like, guilt. In particular, physically touching these items creates strong feelings that make it hard to let go. Understand that it is about so much more than the physical trinkets that clutter their homes and live in boxes in their basements. To part with sentimental items can feel disrespectful to a beloved person or part of one's past.

SENTIMENTALITY SUMMARIZED

Common Phrases	How it Feels	Practical Suggestions
"This was my mom's." "It is too important to let go." "That was a gift from a friend and I feel bad getting rid of it." "I've collected these for years." "It was so important to her."	Connection to past, traditions, culture, or people Can be accompanied by grief, guilt, fear, overwhelm, etc. Conflict between physical object and feeling it elicits Distracted by "memory lane"	Find positive memories Keep things that they enjoy seeing and/or using Shorter sessions Part with unwanted gifts Divide collections and sets Repurpose items Create physical limitations

HOW SENTIMENTALITY FEELS

Most clients express some degree of sentimentality. Clients often say that they avoid deciding about sentimental things because they end up overcome with emotion or distracted, spending hours on memory lane with few results or decisions made. An organizer can be a compassionate listener, but also a gentle nudge to refocus and continue.

Memorabilia was a challenge for my client Christine. She saved all of her two daughters' papers: every drawing, every note, every school paper, every scribble since they were infants. (As any parent can appreciate, young children generate a massive amount of paper.) Now nine and eleven, Christine had several bins of her girls' papers stacked in her bedroom. "I feel so crowded in here, but I don't know what else to do with all their work. Whenever I try to go through it, I either can't decide what to get rid of or the girls are in here and want me to keep everything. I don't even open them anymore because I know I won't be able to do anything," Christine told me.

We set a goal of having only two bins per daughter. Luckily, the bins were already divided by child, so we decided to work first on Anna's. Christine closed her eyes and took a deep breath to ready herself before we opened the first box. The very first picture brought out a long "Awww!" from Christine. It was Anna's drawing of a mermaid underwater. Christine smiled as she looked at the picture. "Anna used to draw mermaids like this. There's probably a thousand of them in here," Christine said with excitement as she dove into the box again.

The next several pieces were much more mundane—penmanship practice and coloring sheets—which Christine flipped through quickly.

"I noticed that you had a big reaction to the mermaid picture, but not so much to these others. What's the difference?" I asked.

"That one reminded me about how she used to draw mermaids. Gosh, she was so into mermaids at that age," Christine said reminiscently. "It just reminds me of when she was little."

"The others don't feel the same way?" I asked.

"Oh, they do! But this one," Christine said as she pointed to the mermaid with her brow furrowed, "I don't know. She made that, so it's special."

"Do you think it would be helpful to sort these? Maybe we could make one pile of pictures, one pile of letters, and we can see what other categories we find?" I asked.

Christine agreed and we set to work on the rest of the box. The box brought out a lot of sighs and smiles from Christine. Occasionally she would stop to tell me a story about a project or drawing or report card. I listened while I continued to sort the papers to keep us moving. Christine was surprised when we reached the bottom of the box in about twenty minutes. "I don't think I've ever gone through an entire box before!" she said. I reminded Christine that we only did the easy part. We still hadn't made any decisions to get rid of anything yet.

We sorted Anna's box of papers from when she was about six or seven years old into categories: penmanship practice, school workbook sheets, tests and quizzes, drawings, coloring, notes, and projects. I asked Christine to look at each category individually.

"Let's look at the coloring pages. Are there any in here that you really like or feel particularly attached to?" I asked.

Christine thumbed through the pile and began to pull out the pages that felt special to her. When she finished, she raised her eyebrows and said to me, "I don't know why I kept so many of these. A lot of them are just scribbling. They felt so important at the time, but now . . ." She shrugged her shoulders as her words trailed off.

"It's okay that you feel differently now." I picked up the few special pieces that she pulled from the pile. "These are the important ones, but they were buried in that box. Knowing that these are your favorites, does that make it easier to let the others go?"

"Yes," Christine said with confidence. "I didn't even know most of what was in there, and I'm sure the kids don't remember either. These," she said as she held up the selected few, "are enough."

We repeated this process with the other categories. Some were easy, like the workbook and writing practice sheets. Others were harder, like the drawings and notes, those things that showed her children's creativity or individuality. But as she saw them grouped together, it allowed Christine to find the special ones. By choosing the best pieces from each category, the memorabilia became a truly curated collection of her kids' pasts.

While I can help my clients sort through and organize sentimental items, those with the most success also address these feelings of sentimentality with a mental health professional. As we work together to sort, purge, and organize, memories and feelings are brought to the surface as happens so vividly when dealing with physical things. My work is in this physical realm. As mental health professionals help navigate the feelings that surface during organizing work, it allows the client to have more perspective, clarity, and confidence to make decisions about what to do with the physical things. As their mind clears, so does their space.

ADDRESSING CLUTTER CAUSED BY SENTIMENTALITY

Positive Memories

When a client considers whether or not to keep a sentimental item, I ask them to tell me about the memories tied to it. With all sentimental objects, I encourage my clients to look for the positive memories. A happy piece of memorabilia has a magical power to instantly link the holder to a moment in the past. Always surprising, though, is how often I hear neutral or even unhappy stories about memorabilia.

> *A happy piece of memorabilia has a magical power to instantly link the holder to a moment in the past.*

I helped my long-time friend, Kristen, sort through some boxes in her basement recently and was puzzled when in one box I found a bag of broken glass pieces.

"Kris, why do you have this bag of glass?" I asked, confused.

She peeked into the bag and said, "Oh, those are the pieces of my mother's vase." She frowned and continued. "I had it on the bookshelf in the living room a few years ago. The kids were fooling around and bumped into the bookshelf and the vase fell and broke. I was so mad at them. I loved that vase," she said sadly. "Mark (her husband) was going to try to put it back together for me, but it would never look the same."

This piece of memorabilia didn't make my friend happy. When she saw that bag, instead of remembering the positive memory of the vase, she thought about how angry she was that it broke, even years later.

Knowing an item's backstory is an important consideration for what sentimental items to keep. Some clients keep things simply because they are part of their past or previously owned by someone else without regard for the item's story. When there isn't a strong history of the item, one that truly resonates, it is important to ask, "Why do you keep this?" or, "Would this be more meaningful to someone else?" Sometimes sharing the item with someone else who would appreciate or value it more is a perfect solution.

In those boxes in Kristen's basement, we found tons of family photographs that dated back to the late 1800s. Kristen wasn't sure what to do with them, but they a were treasure trove for her brother who studied their family's history!

Grief

Grief is one of the strongest causes of sentimental attachment. These feelings often surface when a client attempts to go through sentimental objects at home. Even the volume of objects and the subsequent feelings of overwhelm can leave a client paralyzed. When clients are asked about the types of sentimental items they have at home, you get a more complete picture of the influence of grief.

> *When clients are asked about the types of sentimental items they have at home, you get a more complete picture of the influence of grief.*

Working on items tied to grief is particularly exhausting for clients. I recommend a shorter session of no more than two hours, or to only work on sentimental items for a portion of longer sessions. The mental weight of these items tends to leave clients mentally and emotionally drained. At these sessions, I set up the expectations that it will be difficult to do this work, that they may experience a range of emotions, and that I will not make them get rid of anything. My role is to guide the client with questions and support, so they can make the decisions that are right for themselves.

It's important for you to consider the sentimental objects your clients have in their homes because these objects can create such strong and powerful emotions. My client, Dawn, began to physically shake when she found her deceased husband's wallet unexpectedly in a drawer. It was so difficult for her to touch this reminder of him several years after his death. Although unearthed during organizing work in their homes, these physical links to their pasts conjure memories and feelings that are best addressed by a mental health professional.

> *Although unearthed during organizing work in their homes, these physical links to their pasts conjure memories and feelings that are best addressed by a mental health professional.*

Gifts and Gratitude

The gift-giving process is deeply ingrained in our culture. Gifts are given to celebrate occasions such as birthdays and holidays, to show appreciation, and as rewards. Received gifts can be particularly distressing. Nearly everyone has been given a gift that they don't particularly want or like, but keep because they feel bad getting rid of it.

Unwanted gifts are often kept because of the relationship between the giver and receiver. Challenge clients to think about that relationship as they decide if they can part with a gift. After asking why they received the gift and who gave, it ask:

- How would the giver feel knowing that you struggle so much to decide whether or not to keep this?

- Would this gift be given to you in the first place if the giver knew that you wouldn't use it and would feel guilty about getting rid of it?

- Do you think this gift was given with the intention of creating a negative experience for you?

Often, the client responds that the giver would not want them to be distressed about the gift. With this perspective, it can be easier to let things go. Gifts are given to enjoy. And if you don't enjoy them, you don't need to keep them. Once a gift is given, it's yours to decide whether or not to keep it. Sometimes this is a matter of a client giving themself permission to let it go.

The common rebuttal is, "So-and-so will notice that I don't have such-and-such out anymore," or, "What if Aunt Bertha asks me about that salad bowl she gave me?" Have you ever been in someone's home and asked them to show you some particular gift you gave them? Likely not. Many times, the receiver puts a higher value on the gift than the giver does! Of course, occasionally a client will say that Aunt Bertha does ask about those things. The true value in the gift-giving exchange is in the thoughtfulness of the gift giver and the appreciation of the gift receiver. And often, honesty is the best policy when faced with a question about a gift. The gift receiver can be very appreciative of the time, effort, money, and thought someone else put in to choose a gift. If the gift is truly loved, that is wonderful, but if not, that doesn't minimize the giver's thoughtfulness.

Collections and Sets

A collection is a group of similar items that are carefully researched, curated, preserved, and displayed over time. Collections can be the client's own, either current or from the past, or one that they inherit from someone else. If a collection is received from someone else, the client may not have interest in the collection, but appreciates the time, effort, and reverence the giver put into it. There may even be a financial concern that the collection has a monetary value. When a collection has been given this much care and attention, and when the collection provides positive memories, it has true sentimental value.

Very rarely do I see true collections though. The "collections" my clients tend to have are a multitude of dolls that their now-grown daughter left behind, various vases they have amassed, or items that may be of a similar category, such as books, that weren't carefully curated, but instead are the result of steady acquisition without thought to occasionally weed out.

An interesting aspect of collections is when things are part of a set, but not a true, thoughtful collection. For example, a matching couch, loveseat, and chair in a living room are a collective group of similar things that is referred to as a set. Sets have the same challenges as collections. For many clients, collections (or sets) are seen as one large thing instead of their individual parts. "That's my living room set," or, "This is my model car collection" refers to all parts as one whole. For either of these, a true or amassed collection or set, take a divide and conquer approach.

Morgan collected snow globes from the time she was a child. It was always her souvenir of choice whenever her family traveled. She liked to watch the snowflakes and glitter swirl in their round glass domes. Over time, her extended family and friends began to bring back snow globes for Morgan as gifts. When I worked with Morgan to pack up her childhood bedroom as she prepared to move into her first apartment, the collection was quite large. Although Morgan's intention was to move the whole collection, I noticed she packed certain snow globes more carefully than others. I asked her about why she was more careful with some. She replied, "Well, I didn't buy those. Other people brought them back from their vacations for me." So, the value wasn't necessarily in the snow globe itself. The value was in her experience from that place. I mentioned this to Morgan and she was resistant at first. Because some were gifts, she felt bad not keeping them. And for others, she simply liked how they looked.

Ultimately, we divided the snow globes into three categories: snow globes from her personal travel, snow globes she just liked to look at, and everything else. Once we reviewed and divided the collection into separate categories, Morgan was able to make choices about the three smaller groups. In her new apartment, she displayed the travel snow globes together—a true collection of her experiences and memories. The ones she simply thought were beautiful were used in various places throughout the apartment as decor. And the ones that didn't hold the same sentimental value were donated to her local thrift shop.

Another client, June, inherited a collection of decorative bells from her mom. The collection was lovingly displayed at her mom's home until her passing. Many of the bells had stories associated with them and many family members each had their favorites. Instead of taking the whole collection of bells for herself, she gave each of her mom's family members one bell. In this way, she shared the memory, and the memorabilia, of her mom.

Even simpler sets can be divided. When downsizing, my client Amy knew that she couldn't fit her three-piece living room set into her new house. Her intention was to try to sell the set and purchase something new for the new house. We discussed some configurations of the furniture and realized that the couch and chair would comfortably fit without the loveseat. At first, Amy balked. She couldn't separate them to discard the loveseat only because "they were a set!" Just because things came together doesn't necessarily mean they have to stay together. Dividing the set allowed Amy to repurpose her existing furniture and saved her the time and expense to sell them and purchase new pieces.

Create Physical Limitations

Some sentimental items are not those that would be comfortable on display or used in everyday life. Childhood diaries, wedding dresses, and decades old children's artwork come to mind. For these types of items, it helps to create a physical boundary for how much of these items is saved. Again, this is subjective. There is no right or wrong size, or amount, that can or should be kept. The limitation is a function of the client's comfort level and available space. For many clients, a plastic eighteen-gallon storage bin for such memorabilia is enough. Having a place to collect pieces of the sentimental past is helpful since it creates a designated home for these items. When this bin is full, the client then has to choose. In order to add something new to the container, something else must be removed. This allows for a continuous curating of the person's most important memorabilia.

Everyone experiences attachment to some physical object at one time or another, so it's easy to be empathic to sentimental feelings. Many clients also experience feelings that may not be as obvious as sentimentality. Clients may be less aware of and/or ready to verbalize more covert feelings such as fear and indecision.

CHAPTER 13

"What if I need that one day?" Feelings of Fear

APPRECIATE THE RARE CLIENT who outright says, "I'm scared to do this." Most usually aren't as forthright about the feeling. Many aren't even aware of feeling this way, but they know they are nervous or anxious to call me or start our work together. I sense my clients' fear when they face the clutter and disorganization in their homes: fear they will lose an important part of their past, fear they will make the wrong decisions, fear they aren't competent enough to make the changes they seek, or fear they won't have the necessary resources (i.e., ability, support, finances, etc.).

HOW TO IDENTIFY FEAR

A change in any aspect of life can be scary. I watch for signs that clients are nervous, anxious, or fearful: a jittery tone, fidgeting, excessive talking, or shutting down and avoiding a topic or area of work.

Listen for phrases that start with "What if . . . " and "I can't . . . " I call fear the what-if feeling. *What if* I do this wrong? *What if* I get rid of something I need? *What if* I realize I missed something important? *What if* I can't maintain it once we're done? Clients who experience this fear tend to focus on the possible negative outcomes.

FEAR SUMMARIZED

Common Phrases	How it Feels	Practical Suggestions
"I'm scared to do this." "What if . . . " "I can't . . . "	Debilitating Physical Response Anxiety	Create calm and patient tone Acknowledge feeling and source Answer the "what if" Set focus and goals Create certainty

HOW FEAR FEELS

Fear is one of the more visceral feelings in organizing sessions. Clients show many physical and verbal signs of this emotion. The uncertainty and anxiety of fear causes some clients to panic as we work together. It can feel debilitating and often runs concurrent with other emotions, which makes it even more complicated. To counter this, I create an atmosphere of calm and patience with a slower pace and softer tone. I remind clients of the goal we've set and how they will achieve it, so they can feel powerful and in control.

ADDRESSING CLUTTER CAUSED BY FEAR

Clients gain control and power over their fear when they address the physical stuff. To do this I help them answer the what-ifs, create a focus, and develop tools to counter their uncertainties.

Answer the What-If

Thinking through what-if questions makes the client contemplate the possible and probable scenarios they fear. Based on their responses, they can create the next action or plan. This creates control because it gives them options for how to handle the next step.

Dawn's husband, Patrick, died suddenly a few years ago and she still hadn't touched most of his things. Dawn wanted to move into a smaller, more manageable home since her grown children had moved out. We worked together to downsize and decide what would move on with Dawn. As we worked our way through the house, it was emotional for Dawn. Every room and item held a memory since it was her home with her husband and they raised their family there.

Many of the areas we worked on brought out Dawn's what-if questions. Patrick's clothes still hung in their shared closet and Dawn finally felt ready to remove them. But that didn't mean she was ready to part with them entirely.

"My daughter talked about making a quilt with some of Patrick's shirts. What if she wants some of these?" Dawn asked with concern.

"Well, what if she does?" I asked with soft inquisition.

"I'd have to put them aside for her, but I don't know which ones she'd want." Dawn said, frustrated.

"Are there any here that you want as memorabilia? Any that are particularly meaningful to you?" I asked.

"Just the red plaid one. He wore that a lot." Dawn said as she picked up the shirt. She ran the soft sleeve between her fingers.

I paused a moment before asking, "Are there any that you don't want in the quilt?"

"Well, anything stained, I guess. That wouldn't look nice," she said.

We put the red plaid shirt aside, since we knew that one was special to Dawn. Together, we removed any shirts that Dawn wouldn't want in the quilt, anything with stains, or exceptionally plain ones. The remainder was about twenty shirts. We put them in a box labeled *Dad's Shirts for Kim to Review*.

"Do you know when you'll see Kim next to give her the box?" I asked.

Dawn sighed. "I don't know. She's been so busy lately. What if she's not ready for them? And her apartment is so small, I don't want them to be in her way."

"What if she's not ready for them?" I asked. "Are you willing to hold onto the box for her until she is ready?"

With another sigh Dawn said, "I'd really rather not. My kids tend to leave things here indefinitely. That's one reason I need so much help going through all this stuff now."

"Can we text Kim to ask what she wants to do? At least then we'll know if she is ready for them or not," I asked.

"Absolutely, let me get my phone," she replied.

We went through what-if questions in every room as we worked together over several months: *What if the kids want these baby toys for their own kids? What if I missed an account in Richard's name and it is still open? What if I need this furniture for my new house?* The answers weren't always easy because Dawn couldn't know definitively what would happen. But we answered the initial what-if and probed a little deeper so she could at least take action based on what she thought was likely to happen. In some cases, she even got outright answers—*What if the kids want these baby toys for their own kids?* Dawn kept them because she thought the kids might want them. Simply asking gave her the answer. Neither James nor Kim wanted them. Out they went.

Create a Focus

An end goal for the space creates a focal point for the client. *What is the purpose of this room? How do you want it to function? How do you want to feel in this space?* These questions and their answers lay the foundation for what things need to be (or not be) in that space to reach those goals. When a client struggles, they can come back to the goal of the space to remind themselves what the end benefit will be.

> *What is the purpose of this room? How do you want it to function? How do you want to feel in this space?*

Once the goals for the space are established, the work begins to decide what items to bring into or keep in the space. If the goal of a bedroom is rest and relaxation, the aim is to only keep items in the room that support that goal. This may mean that laundry doesn't come into the room until it is already folded and ready to be put away. Or the bed is made first thing in the morning to create a routine to preserve the calm look of the room.

Focusing on something larger than the individual item gives the client a better perspective since the goal is the priority: *What function does this serve? Does it bring you closer to or farther from your goal(s)?*

> ## What function does this serve? Does it bring you closer to or farther from your goal(s)?

Create Certainty

Because a lot of fear is based in uncertainty (such as the what-ifs), routines are used to create familiarity and structure. It's comforting to know the process for something, what is going to happen, and what the result will be. As an organizer, I model this for my clients. I have the same routine at the beginning of each session. We review what we worked on last time, talk about any questions or concerns that have come up since then, review any homework, and make a plan for the current session. The end of each sessions works similarly: review what we accomplished that day, review any to-do or homework items they have, and set up a preliminary plan for the next sessions. This routine takes a lot of the anxiety out of our work. Clients know what comes next and the steps to get there. In this way, routines are successful because they *remove* questions.

It took all of Cathy's courage to reach out to me about the papers that took over her home office. Visibly shaken, Cathy's voice quivered and her hands fidgeted when we first met.

"I almost cancelled with you today," Cathy said at our first meeting. "I've never shown this to anyone. It's so embarrassing." It was scary for Cathy to bring someone into her home to see this part of her life. She was afraid of judgment, the process, and of feeling guilty and ashamed.

"I understand how scary this can be," I reassured her. "Let's take a look and then we can chat."

All paper was difficult for Cathy, but incoming mail was particularly stressful. Cathy was keenly aware of her fear though. "I get so nervous going through the mail. I know I don't do well staying on top of it, so when I do it, I'm always afraid that there will be something I missed or something I was supposed to do," she explained. Cathy brought the mail in every day, but left it in random piles throughout the house. In an effort to clean up she would collect the piles into a brown paper shopping bag, but that was the end of her system. In her home office, at least ten bags lined the wall near her desk.

Within seconds Cathy started to ramble, "I'm not even sure you can help. I mean, this is just so much. How could we even get through it all? And it never stops! Every day there's more mail. Do I just throw it all out and start fresh?" Cathy paused for a quick breath. "You must think I'm crazy. Who lets it get like this?"

Cathy was spiraling into a frenzy. I had to remove some of her uncertainty. How would I react to her situation? With compassion, understanding, and knowledge. How would the process work? Uniquely tailored to her needs to find out what wasn't working, create systems that would, and teach her the tools to get and stay organized in the future. How would we make sense of all that paper? One piece at a time.

We needed to work on the problem at its source: incoming mail. Cathy needed a plan, a routine, so she would know what to do with the mail as it came in. Over a few sessions we built the routine for the incoming mail—all while also sorting through those ten bags of old mail. First, we made small foundation habits, with the first goal to simply have new mail go into an inbox every day. This was to ensure that nothing was lost and everything was contained to prevent it from becoming more clutter. At the next session we sorted out junk mail and advertisements before mail went into the inbox. Once those skills were part of Cathy's routine, we opened everything relevant and discarded extra pieces of paper, such as outer envelopes and solicitation inserts. Then we batched similar actions together, like *Calls to Make*, *Bills to Pay*, etc. Finally, we set a time each week for Cathy to process the mail in the inbox on her own, which felt very manageable to her.

This step-by-step process empowered Cathy because it removed the uncertainty of *What do I do with this?* She no longer had to decide because the routine told her what to do. I didn't ask her to change all of her habits at once or learn a completely new system. We took it one step at a time and built on the previous steps to build her confidence and get Cathy to her goal of paper management. These small steps helped create a sustainable process and that allowed for consistent practice of the routine.

The vast scenarios created by fear are too wide to cover here. Instead, I chose two common subsets of fear: thrift and comfort. Thrift involves being conscientious about the use of resources—not limited to just money. Comfort results from connectedness to items due to attachments and identity.

THRIFT

Thrift means not being wasteful with money or resources. Some clients keep things that they feel have potential value or use—either now or in the future. I appreciate thrift and understand its value. Of course, it's okay to keep some things. I personally cannot stand to throw out gift bags. They are expensive and totally reusable! Thrift begins to cause trouble, though, when the saving begins to interfere with everyday living space.

THRIFT SUMMARIZED

Common Phrases	How it Feels	Practical Suggestions
"That was expensive."	Generational differences	Consider the present purpose
"I might need it one day."	Keeping things for potential use	Consider future purpose
"As soon as I get rid of it, that's when I'll need it."	Concern for financial or other resources	Limit allowed space 20/20 rule
"That's probably worth something."		

Generational Differences

Thrift may correlate with upbringing. I see it more among seniors and the baby boomer generation. They, or their parents, experienced the Great Depression, so thrift was a common lesson in their childhood homes. Sometimes the conversation has to focus on the past and its influence on thrifty tendencies: *Was money tight as a child? What money lessons did you learn growing up? Are there financial concerns now? Is it related to money, or other reasons such as recycling/environmental concerns?* Knowing the causes of someone's thrift helps to better understand their reasons for and concerns about letting go.

Consider the Present

After learning about a client's past and reasons for thrift, I encourage them to think about the present. For example, I ask, "What does it currently cost you to keep these things?" This can be a financial cost if they pay for storage space, a social cost if the saving causes conflict with others, or a safety cost if physical space is overcrowded.

I urge clients to have a purpose for each item they keep and a limit to the space for such things. Personally, I love my reusable gift bags, but I use a medium-size box to hold them. Once the box is full, I have reached capacity for what I can save. To add something new to the reserve means something else has to come out.

Consider Future Purpose

When a client thinks about the future purpose of an item, they have an opportunity to realistically consider their expectations. Shift the thought from *I might need this one day*, to, *What is the likelihood that I will need this in the future?* This gives the client an applicable question that can help them to decide an item's real value. This reframing allows clients to consider the probability, not just possibility, of future need.

The Minimalists suggest a 20/20 technique[46] in situations like these. When in doubt about whether or not to keep something, consider if that item can be replaced for less than twenty dollars and in less than twenty minutes. Acknowledging that something can be replaced quickly with low cost can make the decision to let go much easier. For example:

Is this third extension cord really needed?

Well, a run to Walmart will take less than twenty minutes and a new cord will cost less than twenty dollars.

These small time and money investments help give perspective to some decisions about whether to keep or let go.

It is also important for clients to be honest about how much they really keep for use "someday." "In case the kids want it," or, "If we move," or, "When I get around to . . . " are all reasons to save things. But does that economical reason encroach on today's life?

Without fail, whenever I work with a client in a kitchen, at least once I hear, "Why do I have so much Tupperware?" Jane was no different. A single mom who lived with her daughter, Nicole, Jane hired me to help tame her kitchen clutter and create systems so the space could be used more efficiently. In multiple cabinets we found small stockpiles of plastic food containers. And, of course, there were more lids than bottoms. (Why does that happen?) Some were good quality matching sets. Others were various sizes, styles, and depths. And many were recycled from takeout dinners.

I asked Jane, "Why are there so many?"

"It seems wasteful to throw them out. We do reuse them. And sometimes you need a particular size. And I want some that Nicole can take to school and I don't mind if they don't come back."

Jane had to chuckle at herself when I asked, "Would it be possible for you to ever use all of these at once?" Of course, she couldn't.

I understood Jane's reasoning. She wanted to be financially and environmentally conscious and she did use them, but the volume created a logjam. They were in multiple places because she couldn't fit them all in one spot. It was frustrating to find matching lids and the varying sizes meant many didn't stack neatly.

We gathered all of the containers together on the counter and I asked Jane to pick out her favorite ones, the ones she and Nicole used most often, and made sure each had a matching lid. We looked at her kitchen and decided that a lower cabinet next to her refrigerator made the most sense to store these containers. It was a wide cabinet with two shelves and her favorites would only fill about half of one shelf. I asked Jane if she felt comfortable using this cabinet as a boundary for the plasticware. She could keep what fit in this cabinet, but no more. She was hesitant at first, but finally agreed. We arranged her favorites and their lids so that she and Nicole could easily grab them.

But we still had all the extra containers on the counter. I asked Jane to imagine she had a big dinner party. "Imagine at the end of the party you had a lot of leftovers you wanted to store. Which of these ones left would you use?" Jane talked about which sizes were good and which were sturdier. She pulled out about six or seven more pieces that she deemed worthy to go into the cabinet. Jane also said that sometimes she likes to have a few containers for odd tasks, like soaking a piece of laundry. She pulled out two more pieces and they went into the cabinet too, which was now full. About half of the containers were still on the counter, but these pieces were less important to Jane, were random bottoms or lids, or were ones Jane couldn't see herself using in the future. These all went into recycling.

By designating a spot, we created a physical boundary. This was where plastic food containers go. If Jane wanted to add something, something else must come out. This process made Jane think about how she actually used her things and her space and think about how she was likely to use them in the future. Pieces that didn't fit, both literally and figuratively, were removed. Jane used a more limited space, but it was also less overwhelming since each piece had a purpose and helped fulfill her goal of a more functional kitchen.

COMFORT

Attachment to things can come from a need for comfort or security. As shown with the psychological home, attachment to items either links someone to their past or creates that person's individuality. These attachments bring a sense of comfort created by the object(s). When faced with parting with them, there is a fear of loss of either the sense of security that item brings or fear of loss of the personal self.

COMFORT SUMMARIZED

Common Phrases	How it Feels	Practical Suggestions
"If I put it away, I won't know where to find it." "Oh, I've had that forever." "I like my things. They make me feel at home."	Attachment for security or sense of self Totality brings comfort	Collect like items together Clear storage options for containment

Comfort can be a difficult attachment since parting with these things conflicts with their perceived purpose. It is the total of all these things that brings comfort. It is important to explore this connection to understand why this fear manifests in physical things. Since reducing the amount of these things is so difficult, it's usually best to contain them in an orderly way.

Collect Like Items Together

Grouping is a basic organizing technique that works particularly well with comfort struggles. Grouping brings all like items together into categories that make sense to the client. Again, the subjectivity of organizing is important here. Different clients will create different categories for the same types of items. For example, the table below shows how three different clients may group clothes into different categories:

Client 1	Client 2	Client 3
Short sleeve shirts Long sleeve shirts Pants Shorts	Work Casual Going out Workout	Base layer Shirts Sweaters/Blazers Work Bottoms Casual Bottoms Loungewear

No one way is right or wrong, better or worse than any other. The most important thing is that the categories resonate with the client.

Olivia's mom wanted someone to help Olivia organize her bedroom. Olivia was a busy teen: school, sports, activities, and social life. One of Olivia's passions was running. She began running at age ten, and now competed fiercely on her high school track team. She had hundreds of medals, trophies, and race bibs from her years of races and meets. All these accolades were strewn everywhere in her room. Medals hung from her four-poster bed. Race bibs littered her desk and dresser top. Trophies were stashed in random places throughout her room and closet. Olivia felt very attached to these reminders of her accomplishments and expressed doubt that she would want to part with any of them.

My first step with Olivia was to gather all the track memorabilia together and then group them into categories. "If we sort all of this into groups, what categories would you make?" I asked Olivia.

She looked confused. "I don't know. They're all just track," she said.

I picked up two random race bibs. "So, for example, are these two bibs the same to you? When you think about track, are they both equally important?"

Olivia looked at each bib. "Well, they're both important, but this one is from a one-mile race and this is from a 10K, so they aren't the same."

"Does that make a difference to you? Would you want them separate?" I asked.

For Olivia, it made sense to make groups based on the distance of the race (1-miler, 5K, 10K). Once these groups were together, Olivia told me about each. More than just the distance of the race was significant to Olivia. The one-mile races were from when she first started running. She remembered feeling so proud that she was in a "real" race back then. She showed me notes she scribbled on the back of some of the race bibs to show the date, a time, and PR! PR was her personal record. She had similar notes on the longer distance bibs too. As we continued looking through each category,

Olivia occasionally came across a medal or trophy and couldn't remember the race. She had done so many. She still wanted to keep them, though, because it represented something she had done, even if she couldn't remember it. The trophies, medals, and bibs were a way to show her commitment to and progress through her sport. Olivia felt it was important for her to see these reminders of her accomplishments, both to feel proud of herself and to encourage her to continue to achieve.

We did find a way to showcase her track memorabilia. We hung three specialty plaques designed to hold race bibs and medals, one for each race distance. Over each plaque hung a picture frame with the bib with Olivia's current personal record for each. There were far fewer trophies than we expected and we installed one new shelf to neatly hold them all. We created a way for Olivia to keep this memorabilia and showcase it. It became a proud display of her accomplishments instead of random clutter throughout her room.

Use Clear Storage

Early in my career, if a client said to me, "If I put it away, I won't be able to find it," I would freeze. How could we possibly leave everything out? But I also understood the concern about losing track of something if the client didn't have the visual reminder. I learned that these visual cues were extremely important to some people. The challenge was to make sure that everything being out didn't turn into a landscape of clutter that they glossed over visually. Have you ever experienced that? Not realizing something was in an awkward or inconvenient place simply because that was where it had always been?

Clear storage options are very helpful in these situations. Clear bins allow clients to categorize and contain, but still be able to see what is inside so things don't feel hidden. It makes things organized and accessible and satisfies their visual need. This is particularly helpful for clients who have collections of things like crafting supplies. Crafters often have various items for different projects. And many times, they want to have just what they need on hand. This kind of bin allows for the randomness and creativity that makes their crafts so unique and special, but also creates a sense of order in their space.

Paper tends to be another "I'm leaving it out so I remember to do it" item. And with the daily influx of mail, paper becomes overwhelming very quickly. Here, clear storage solutions and a processing routine work wonders. (Of course, the first tip always is to eliminate any junk mail before it lands in the house. Recycle flyers and solicitations right away!) For clients who like to leave out paper reminders, they can try clear poly paper jackets. These are similar to plastic folders except they only open on the top and one side to create a pocket. Label the pockets by action like *Calls to Make, Errands to Run, Bills to Pay*. When mail comes in, or needs to be cleared off a desk or counter, papers are easily sorted into these pockets. Then similar tasks, such as phone calls, are all together. Even if these poly jackets stay out on a desk as a visual reminder, the paper is contained but visible.

When clients answer the what-ifs, focus on their ultimate goals, and create routines, they can use these tools to overcome the feelings of fear created by either their stuff or the prospect of decluttering.

CHAPTER 14

"I don't have time."
Feelings of Indecision

NDECISION ISN'T ONLY NOT MAKING A CHOICE. Sometimes it's the inability to make a choice. What is in the home, how money is spent, how time is spent—these are all decisions. When clients struggle with indecision, they feel they either have too many options or not enough. Too many options feels overwhelming, but not having enough options feels like any decision may not be the best choice.

So, couldn't indecision also be described as procrastination? Eventually, things have to get done, whether the best solution is found or not. Isn't not deciding actually deciding not to decide? Yes, indecisiveness can also be called decisional procrastination.

Ferrari and Roster looked at this connection in their article "Delaying Disposition: Examining the Relationship between Procrastination and Clutter Across Generations." They defined *Decisional procrastination* as, "a maladaptive tendency to postpone decisions when faced with conflicts or choices."[47] They found that "general procrastination tendencies may enable a lifelong pattern of responses to one's environment that become increasingly maladaptive throughout the life cycle - simultaneously delaying disposal decisions."[48] Basically, indecision about clutter creates even more clutter.

Basically, indecision about clutter creates even more clutter.

The Relationship of Procrastination and Clutter

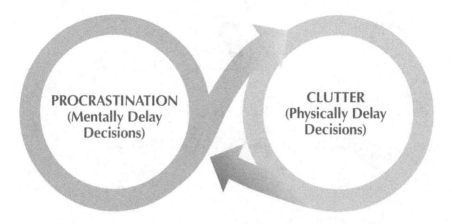

PROCRASTINATION
(Mentally Delay
Decisions)

CLUTTER
(Physically Delay
Decisions)

The simplest definition of clutter is delayed decisions. This is another example of how the physical and mental worlds mirror each other. To mentally delay decisions is procrastination. To physically delay decisions creates clutter. Procrastination leads to clutter. And the more clutter there is, the harder it is to make decisions, which leads to more procrastination. It's one layer of the cyclical relationship between minds and stuff.

What do I do with this? How will I get rid of this? Where do I start? How long will it take? What if I can't finish in time? What if someone else wants that? How can I find the time? What if it doesn't fit? These questions fill clients' minds. Because the answers are not always clear, it can be difficult for them to move forward and make decisions.

This indecision creates the client's rationale for why they haven't gotten organized, now or in the past. As Dr. Ferrari writes, "Because dispositional decisions can be stressful, especially for individuals who form close attachments to their possessions, indecisives may avoid disposal tasks because they are afraid of making the wrong decision or regretting their actions later."[49]

But to simply not decide isn't productive, preferred, or sometimes even possible. If clutter negatively affects a client's life, decisions have to be made for change to happen. And these decisions don't just apply to the physical objects. Clients have to decide how they will incorporate these changes into their daily lives and schedules, if they are ready to invest financially in professional help, and how they will maintain motivation and momentum. In the scope of decision-making, the objects themselves might be the smallest decisions to make.

Indecisive clients were a struggle for me at first. If a client paid for expertise, I felt unqualified if I couldn't immediately deliver. I felt I should have all the answers to all their questions.

I've since learned that I can have lots of knowledge and experience and still not have the perfect answer. Since each organizing situation is different, a new and unique solution needs to be found every time. While I can pull from my knowledge of products and organizing principles and make a best guess at a good solution, to find a great solution I need the client's help.

When Theresa called, she was frantic. "My kitchen is being renovated in four weeks. I don't even know where to start to get ready, but I know things are chaotic here and it's only going to get worse," she said in one long breath. The deadline was her great motivator.

An emergency room nurse and mom of three kids ranging in age from ten years to ten months, Theresa had a lot going on. Her husband, Michael, worked in Philadelphia with a two-hour commute each way every day. "I want to be here to help more, but by the time I get home, the kids are just about done for the day and we're both exhausted too," Michael said.

"We shuffled bedrooms when the baby was born. I gave my oldest the office, so now all of that is in here," Theresa said as we walked into the family room. "Maybe in here is where we need to work since that will be the main place for us to hang out when the kitchen is being redone. It's just stressful in here now, and if this is where we're going to be, it needs to work better," Theresa mused. Then she paused, lost in thought for a moment. "Although the living room probably needs work too, since that's on the main floor that's where the baby usually is. But I don't know where any of that stuff would go unless we work on the basement and the closets, but those are full too. This is part of the reason I called you. I know we need help, but I don't even know with what!"

I asked some questions about the use of the living and family rooms and their goals before we went to the kitchen so I could see that space too. Theresa bubbled with excitement as she told me about the how the space would be redesigned, complete with removing the wall between the kitchen and dining room and reconfiguring the cabinets and appliances.

"It sounds amazing!" I said, impressed with the thoughtfulness they put into the new design. "Have you thought about a setup for a makeshift kitchen while the work is being done?"

I watched Theresa's eyes go wide. "Oh, I didn't even think of that! I knew we wouldn't be able to use the kitchen, but I didn't really think about what that would mean day-to-day," Theresa said, exasperated.

Michael chimed in. "The plumbers have to move some pipes downstairs. Everything in the basement along these walls," he said as he pointed to the left and back walls of the kitchen, "needs to be moved so the plumbers can run the new pipes."

Theresa's face dropped and she held back tears. "I didn't even think of that either. What are we . . . How are we . . . There's so much stuff down there!" She buried her face in her hands. "They're going to be here to start in four weeks! We don't have time to do all this! And if we pull everything out of the kitchen *and* the basement, we won't be able to move in here. There's just not enough space. I don't know how we are going to do this," she said, crestfallen.

When I first started my business, this would drive me crazy. *Just decide!* I would scream in my head! I felt clients were just making excuses to rationalize not taking action. *Just decide when you will do it. Just decide how. And then do it!* I cringe at my old attitude. I've learned that my client's lives are a constant tussle between when and how. I had to help Theresa and Michael figure those out.

In a steady and serious voice, I said, "Let's start at the beginning. What needs to be done before the demo starts?"

We made a master list of what needed to be done and a created a timeline that worked backward from the project start date. Next, we noted who would be responsible for each task. Theresa could box up the kitchen. Michael could set up the makeshift kitchen. They both had to work on the basement. And finally, we estimated how long each task would take.

Based on their schedules and our timeline, it wasn't realistic for Theresa and Michael to get everything done on their own. They could prepare the kitchen and living room spaces, but the basement would be too much. And Theresa's original priority of the family room was taken off the agenda altogether. They agreed to a team of organizers and assistants to sort, purge, and reorganize the basement. The help with this space allowed them to focus more of their time upstairs.

We used both large chunks on weekends and small pockets of time on weekdays to get things done. Having the time blocked off helped Theresa and Michael stay accountable to their timeline. Each appointment listed exactly which task they were to work on, such as "Pack bottom cabinets," or "Clean out pantry." They didn't have to decide what to work on to move toward their goal. It was already there.

I checked in with Theresa a few weeks into the renovation. It was still chaotic due to the work being done on the house, as expected, but it was manageable. It also gave her the motivation to work on those other areas of her home like the family room. My heart swelled with pride when she said, "I don't feel the pressure to do it all at once anymore. That's just not realistic. But I can accomplish something in five minutes, and over time that adds up."

HOW TO IDENTIFY INDECISION

Indecision makes clients feel frozen. They know that decisions come before any of subsequent actions. It is very frustrating to feel that progress hinges completely on the ability to decide something. And it doesn't happen only in the decision to start. It can happen at any point in the organizing process since decisions are constantly made: where to start, when to stop, what to keep, what to toss, where to store, how to store, etc. Indecision comes across is many ways.

INDECISION SUMMARIZED

Common Phrases	How it Feels	Practical Suggestions
"I don't have time." "My house is too small." "I don't know what to get rid of."	Inability to make choices/Frozen Frustrating Can happen at any point in the organizing process	Schedule time/ Chunking Consider the probable value Judicious purging Three questions

HOW INDECISION FEELS

The process of organizing is exhausting. Clients expect to have sore muscles and hungry bellies at the end of a long organizing day. Less obvious is the mental energy that organizing takes. Every decision to keep, donate, or toss takes mental energy. It is no wonder clients' brains feel tired at the end of the day. The brain gets worn out just like any other muscle. Decision fatigue is common among indecision clients, and it shows itself in slowed decision making, distraction, or even moodiness and outbursts.

ADDRESSING CLUTTER CAUSED BY INDECISION

Make Time

The top indecision phrase I hear is, "I don't have time." Nearly every new client shares how their schedule is more stuffed than their closets. But the truth is that clutter wastes time. Clients waste time looking for things. They constantly shuffle piles around to make room to do things. The home functions inefficiently.

Instead of "finding" the time, clients need to make the time: prioritize it and schedule it. I encourage clients to consider the investment of their time as an investment in themselves, their families, and in their homes. To do this, clients are told to make an appointment with themselves and respect it the same way they would any other appointment. The key here is to be specific. *I'm going to organize the kitchen this weekend,* is not specific enough. Instead, they set the times to start and stop. This becomes, *I'm blocking off an hour at 7:00 p.m. on Friday night,* or, *I'm working on this from 10:00 a.m. to 2:00 p.m. on Saturday.* The amount of time is less important than scheduling it. A set time is helpful in two ways. First, it helps the client get started because it gives them a mental appointment with themselves. This time is blocked off for the task. Second, an end time keeps the client focused. Instead of thinking, *Oh, this is never going to get done,* they can focus on, *I'm going to work on this for two hours.*

It's also important for clients to know that not everything can be done in one appointment. A jam-packed garage will not be completed in two hours. However, two dedicated hours brings a client closer to their end goal and motivates them to schedule the next time to work on it. This is an important time management technique called chunking. Chunking breaks larger projects down into smaller bits. And believe me, the bits can be pretty small. If the client only has fifteen minutes, they can do one box, one drawer, or one shelf. And fifteen minutes every day for a month is seven and a half hours—the same as committing a whole Saturday to the project.

As with Theresa and Michael, they had to make the time in their schedule to prepare for the renovation. This wasn't and couldn't be a large weekend project. The smaller goals set in their calendars allowed them to see their progress every day. And chunking the time into smaller blocks meant that they could make the time every day. As I worked with Theresa and Michael throughout the weeks before the renovation, Theresa was surprised to find that she continued working on the tasks at other times. She told me, "Once I got started, it somehow felt easier to continue. I even looked for ways to get ahead so I could take some days off guilt-free."

Address Home Size

The second most common indecision excuse I hear is, "My house is too small." Everyone says this: from the one-bedroom New York City apartment renters to the sprawling ten-thousand-square-foot suburban homeowners. There is one constant, though—unless there is a plan for an immediate change, such as a move, the amount of space a client has is fixed. Their stuff is variable. While clients can't control how much space they have, short of living somewhere else, they can control how much stuff they have in their space. It is important for clients to consider which has more value: the stuff or how they feel in their space.

> *It is important for clients to consider which has more value: the stuff or how they feel in their space.*

Betty lived in her two-bedroom apartment for about five years. A single woman, she used the second bedroom as a home office for her job with a financial brokerage house. The office also served as a guest room when family stayed with her. Betty called me, mad and frustrated at herself, when she had to refuse a visit because the office had become too cluttered for her relatives to stay.

The office had become the catchall of Betty's apartment. Mail order delivery? She put the box in the office until she was ready to open it. New craft project? The extra supplies lived in the office while she worked on it. Workout equipment that didn't work out? It stayed in the office until she could figure out what to do with it. And even though it felt tight in there, Betty still used it as her home office every day. "I feel so stressed when I walk in here to start work in the morning. It feels claustrophobic. I feel my shoulders tighten as soon as I walk in the door," she told me.

I proposed the "what's more important, the stuff or the space?" question to Betty many times as we worked together: "Are these boxes from Amazon, Etsy, and Chewy more important than feeling good in this space?" "If we simply donated the treadmill would the openness of the room be more valuable than whatever money she could make if she sold it on Craigslist?" "If the craft supplies were important for a valued hobby, could we find a better way to store them so you don't have to look at them every day?" The value of Betty's space became clearer as she answered these questions. It was more important to her to have that space clear for work and ready for visitors. And ı led her to let go of the less important things.

Betty called a few months later to hire me again. This ... was to help her unpack in a new apartment. She enjoyed the new look and feel of the office so much that she continued to use the techniques in other rooms in her apartment over the following few months. She was ready to move into a one-bedroom apartment instead. She told me, "I thought about all the furniture and stuff I had in my apartment and really thought about how it made me feel, how much I used it, and what purpose it was serving. I started letting go of the things that didn't fit my goals and my lifestyle. Soon, my apartment felt so big, too big really. I checked with the leasing office and realized I'm paying an extra three hundred and fifty dollars for the two-bedroom apartment instead of a one-bedroom. Three hundred and fifty dollars a month! I put in a request to move that day."

Clients need to be more judicious about what stays and what can go. There is no easy way around this once they decide to shift their focus to the value of their space over the value of the stuff. But they also often need guidance or parameters for those decisions. Of course, this honest revelation to clients ultimately leads to the question, *How do I decide what can go?*

The Three Questions

I encourage clients to keep things in their homes that have a purpose; are effective, efficient, and useful; and make them feel good. To identify these things, I use three simple questions:

1. **Do you use it?** Everyone has their own most frequently used items. For me, I use my stainless steel Dutch oven for just about every dinner I cook.

2. **Do you need it?** There are certain possessions that are just necessary to keep. Recent tax papers, vital documents, and medical supplies come to mind.

3. **Do you love it?** I have a glass paperweight on my desk that I just love. It isn't expensive or sentimental. I just like how it looks and I enjoy seeing it every day.

A client's answers to these questions help them decide which items to keep. For example, I held up a green blouse to show my client Diane. "How about this shirt? Do you wear this?"

"No, I haven't worn that in forever," Diane responded.

"Is it sentimental or part of a uniform or something?" I asked. "No."

"Last time you wore it, did you love it? Did you feel good wearing it?" I asked.

"No, not really. I don't like how it fits, or the color really," she said.

Diane didn't use this shirt, didn't have a specific need for it, and didn't love to wear it. Out it went!

I held up a different blouse to Diane, this time a light blue one with a geometric pattern. "How about this shirt?"

"Absolutely! I wear that two or three times a month. It's a go-to top for me. And I just love that pattern! Isn't that cool?" Diane responded excitedly. This was a definite keep.

Clients are usually quick to answer on these items and the answers tend to spill out all at once. Diane wore this top frequently and loved how she felt when she wore it.

The third shirt I help up, a white button-down dress shirt, got a different response. "Do you wear this?"

"Sometimes," Diane said thoughtfully. "It's not my favorite, but I do wear it."

"So, you don't love it?" I gently inquired.

"It's okay. I like it, but not love it," she answered.

"Do you have other shirts like this that you would pick first? Or do you wear this for specific outfits?" I asked.

"I wear it with this blazer, but that's it."

In-between pieces are usually the challenge for clients, whether they work with an organizer or on their own. When the answer is an obvious yes or no, the choice is easy. It is more difficult when the answer is less clear because that is when they have to make a decision. To help my clients with this, I put all these "maybe" pieces aside. When we finish the easier choices, we come back to them.

"Diane, I sorted the 'maybes' into categories by type of clothing. Let's compare each to the pieces you've decided to keep to see if they fill any gaps in your wardrobe," I said.

We took the first pile, the blouses from earlier, over to the closet. We looked at the other button-down shirts that Diane decided to keep and she realized that the one in the "maybe" pile isn't that great compared to them.

"I would pick any of these," she said of the "keep" dress shirts in her closet, "over this one. I didn't realize I had so many already. This one can go."

When the answer is yes to one or two of the questions, the client has to consider if the need and/or use of the item outweighs the physical, spatial, and emotional costs to keep it. Sometimes the client has to consider if there is enough room to keep the item. Sometimes it needs to be compared to other similar items to see if it is unique enough to keep, as Diane did. Compare the "maybes" to what are definite "keeps" in order to improve the client's perspective about what they really need, use, and love.

The value of *Do you love it?* should not be underestimated. Keeping things simply because they are enjoyed is absolutely valid. I never use my beautiful glass paperweight to hold down papers. I just enjoy the sight of it on my desk. This is reason enough to keep it.

The process of asking these three questions is slow in the beginning but becomes more natural as it's practiced. When a client answers yes to all three of these questions, that is something to keep. Wouldn't it be amazing if everything in a home is needed, used, and loved? Similarly, when the answer to all three is no, it gives the client the opportunity to reevaluate why that thing is in their home at all.

> *And with practice, the three questions lead them to fill their space with things that add value to their lives.*

Most clients struggle with indecision at some point. Decision-making can cause angst and overwhelm. It takes time and repetition to build confidence in decision-making abilities. When clients understand their control over their time and home size, they can set realistic goals and expectations for their use. And with practice, the three questions lead them to fill their space with things that add value to their lives.

CHAPTER 15

"I don't know where to start."
Feelings of Overwhelm & Defeat

OFTEN COUPLED WITH SENTIMENTALITY, fear, and/or indecision is the feeling of overwhelm. Overwhelm is a universal
emotion in organizing. The sheer volume of stuff, the decisions, and
the process of getting organized can stop a well-intentioned client
in their tracks. Every client experiences it at some point in the process. There are several common reasons for this. One is a new experience. My clients Sarah and Charles called because they moved
into their first apartment together and struggled to "keep up with
having a house." Some may call this "adulting." Another reason is
an unexpected event. John and Susan called because their son was
having surgery and needed to rehabilitate at home. This meant their
house had to be reconfigured to accommodate his needs. Sometimes the reason is that the client has simply fallen into a routine
of "too much." Pam felt her whole life was overwhelming: kids, a
large house, volunteer positions, multiple extracurricular activities
on multiple days of the week. She felt like her life was constantly in
high gear.

When clients experience feelings of overwhelm, it can be par-
alyzing. When there's so much to do, how does one even start? In
professional organizing and in therapy sessions, overwhelm is easily

recognized because clients usually self-identify the feeling. "I feel so overwhelmed" is a phrase often said by my clients at least once during our initial phone call or in-person assessment.

For some clients, the feeling of overwhelm comes from the sheer volume of stuff. Basements, attics, and garages are catchall spots for things they don't make decisions on right away. Most of us can relate to a space full of stuff that has collected over months, years, or even decades. It is understandable that these places create feelings of overwhelm. To tackle these spaces full of who-knows-what feels big and daunting. A client recently said to me about her overstuffed garage, "I see this and I avoid it. I just disengage." One advantage to these storage spaces is that the door can be closed and the clutter and decisions are contained and hidden.

Feelings of overwhelm are more intense and distressing when everyday living spaces are cluttered. When the mess is seen every day, it's harder to ignore or dismiss. One space that is often lower on clients' priority list, but a major source of overwhelm, is the master bedroom. For many, this is where laundry (usually clean, but sometimes dirty) lands. Stacks of to-do items such as returns to make to the store litter the floor. Books and hobbies collect on nightstands and open shelves. Starting and ending the day amidst these stressors undermines the restfulness that one should feel in the place of sleep! When every space in the home feels inefficient, cluttered, or disorganized it can be difficult to know how, or even where, to begin to make changes. As Drs. Ferrari and Roster write, "Individuals who chronically put off organizing and purging tasks may find that their failure to do [so] has created a situation so out of control that they cannot bear the time and effort needed to start the process."[50]

> *When every space in the home feels inefficient, cluttered, or disorganized it can be difficult to know how, or even where, to begin to make changes.*

For others, feelings of overwhelm come from past experiences of trying to clear out and organize their space. If they made efforts in the past and still struggle, it can feel defeating. Home should be a place of sanctuary. Feelings of overwhelm and defeat threaten that sanctuary and instead weigh on people physically, mentally, and emotionally.

Examples of this overwhelm come from all rooms in the house. When the issue intensifies and multiple rooms are involved, clients can feel disgust, both at their surroundings and at themselves. Because overwhelm is such a common reaction to clutter, it is important to have tools at the ready to address overwhelm. Talk therapy is the perfect place to acknowledge the feeling and discuss ways to move past it.

HOW TO IDENTIFY OVERWHELM AND DEFEAT

Overwhelm is easily the most common reason people call for help. Over ninety percent of my clients use the word "overwhelmed" in our first conversation. Others are more covert. While simply saying "overwhelmed" is the most common, I also listen for any way the client suggests that the space or the stuff feels "too big," "too hard," or "too much."

OVERWHELM SUMMARIZED

Common Phrases	How it Feels	Practical Suggestions
"I don't know where to start."	Paralyzing, lonely, impossible	Reframe project to process
"I clear it out and it just gets messy again."	Commonly self-identified	Realistic goal setting and routines
"I feel so frustrated."	Defeated from previous attempts that haven't been sustained	Acknowledge the cause
"Too big/hard/ much."		Commit to change
		Maintenance

HOW OVERWHELM AND DEFEAT FEEL

George's voicemail gave me a lot of clues that he felt overwhelmed by his space. In a tense voice, with lots of sighs and pauses he said:

"Hi, my name is George. I came across your website and I'm wondering if you can help. I just have a lot of stuff and want to clear it out, but, umm, I don't know where to start or what to do or if you can help . . . Our house has a lot of storage space in the basement, but there's a lot of stuff down there. I'm not even sure what some of it is. I mean, we've been through it before and . . . uh, I don't know what happened. Well, it's not just the basement, I guess. It's really, um, the kitchen, maybe, and the playroom, well . . . it's everywhere. It's just a lot. My wife and I both work full time so we'd like to know if you are available on weekends, too. So, if you could call me back at . . ."

Calls like George's are very common. In those initial conversations, callers don't even know where to begin to talk about their space. Some bounce around from this room to that room, this stuff to that stuff, work, kids, home. Their minds must feel as scattered as their spaces. Other callers just freeze, not sure what to say first. For these I say, "Tell me what prompted you to call today."

I feel the most compassion for overwhelmed clients regardless of its cause: the amount of stuff, the buildup of anxiety, or not knowing what step to take next. The sense of helplessness that overwhelm creates is defeating, lonely, and impossible. I make it a point to tell these clients how common overwhelm is. It creates a sense of relief to identify the feeling and know that it's a normal reaction. Knowing that others feel this way, too, makes addressing clutter feel less shameful, embarrassing, and intimidating.

ADDRESSING CLUTTER CAUSED BY OVERWHELM AND DEFEAT

Change the Frame from Project to Process

Clients often refer to their organizing challenge as a project. This suggests that organizing is a "one and done" experience; that there are pre-fabricated solutions to make any space work perfectly. Unfortunately, it doesn't work that way. Instead, clients need to retrain their minds to view the space as a project, but organizing as a whole as a process.

Recall Cathy who felt overwhelmed by paper. The project part of getting organized was to go through the backlog of papers. That was a basic organization piece. However, her mail and paperwork had a continual inflow. Knowing what to do with new pieces of incoming paper, how to process important information, and how to decide what should be saved were all crucial to her long-term organization system. These were the pieces of the organizing process.

Setting goals and building habits are also important parts to getting and staying organized. But these things take time to accomplish. Some organizing clients look for the quick fix to bring order to their space. They want it "Pinterest Perfect." In some cases, this works. For example, a team of organizers unpacking from a move offers quick, efficient results. In most situations, though, the "one and done" approach will look great at first, but won't be a lasting solution since the client didn't learn the steps of the organizing process.

Smaller steps and building on existing habits are all part of the organizing process that results in lasting change.

In most cases, a slower paced approach provides more thoughtful and long-term changes. Clients need to repeat an action thirty times before it becomes a habit. This is thirty days of the mail getting into the designated inbox, thirty house pickups to help with maintenance, thirty times following an evening routine. And often, there are multiple steps to a given process, which makes the learning time even longer. These smaller steps and building on existing habits are all part of the organizing process that results in lasting change.

Nearly every new client wants to know how long it will take to organize a space. An organizer may be able to give an estimate for how long it will take purge, sort, evaluate, and containerize, but "organize" is a fluid and subjective word. Organized is being able to find what you need when you need it. To get to the point of organized takes time and practice. The space did not become disorganized overnight, so it is fair to expect it to take time to regain control and become organized. Shifting the idea of "getting organized" from a project to process is crucial. There is more to consider than the physical stuff. How is the space is used? Who uses the space? What aesthetics are wanted for the room? When clients take a measured approach to this change, they can learn intuitive new habits, build on previous work, and create an environment that sets them up for future success. This view also removes pressure for an immediate change and perfection. Framing organization this way helps set realistic expectations and allows clients to celebrate small victories on the journey.

Deborah is the perfect example of changing the frame. When Deborah first called, she sounded overwhelmed in her words and her tone. She didn't know where to start and wanted everything done at once.

"It's been too long like this, but I don't know how to start," Deborah said.

"What areas do you want to focus on?" I asked.

Deborah sighed and I heard her eyes roll through the phone, "All of them. The kitchen, bedroom, front hall." Each space had its own challenges.

I explained how all the projects she wanted to work on were separate parts of the organizing process. "It's important to consider your home as a whole so that it functions as a cohesive unit. But we can work on one space at a time so that you feel a sense of progress and completion at each stage of our work," I reassured her.

I wanted Deborah to understand the time and effort each space required, so she would have realistic expectations of our work together and of herself. She didn't have to do it all at once. We focused on one shelf, one drawer at a time. We built up momentum and cleared whole rooms and eventually her whole house. The progress was slow at first, but every step was realistic, attainable, and maintainable.

Acknowledge the Cause

One of the main reasons clients need to be hands-on in the organizing process is they have the answers to many of their own organizing challenges, whether they realize it or not. Conversations with clients help identify the root causes of their disorganization. With key questions, the client can discern how a space is used and what causes the clutter hurdles. It is never just about the stuff. It is about the space, who uses it, and the systems in place, all of which can have underlying emotional attachments and triggers.

Take, for example, kitchens. Kitchens are designed to cook and, in some cases, to eat. Low cabinets are designed to hold large pots. The dishwasher is usually set next to the sink for functionality. Top drawers are shallow to accommodate utensils and potholders. Think about, however, how kitchens are used. As a client walks me through their cluttered kitchen, they tell me how there isn't enough counter space and stuff gets shuffled from the counter to the table to the chair and back again. Their complaints usually focus on the cooking and eating done in the kitchen. Everyone says to me with frustration in their voices, "I always have to move things so I can cook," and, "Every day we have to clear the table to have dinner. But then everything gets put on the counter!"

The aha moment comes when I ask, "What else is done in the kitchen?"

"The kids do homework here, and I go through their school papers."

"I pay bills at the table."

"I watch shows on the iPad while I wash dishes."

"The dog's leash is in this drawer."

"The kids play in here while I cook."

This is why many kitchens are disorganized. The kitchen is the hub of nearly every home. They aren't designed or set up for the activities that actually take place there. Kitchens are for cooking and eating, but also for homework and bill paying, grabbing snacks, conversations to catch up on the day or schedule the next, and at every party, the kitchen is the center of activity. Of course, kitchens are cluttered! A room designed for two activities can't be expected to function well for so many more. Once the client acknowledges these uses, it's easier to create spaces and systems that incorporate all these different activities. This could be a drawer dedicated to homework or art supplies so that kids can find (and put away) these things when they use them in the kitchen. It may be a portable bill-paying caddy so that bills can be done at the table, but cleared easily when it's time to eat.

> *Understanding what happens in a space is just as important as what stuff is in there.*

Understanding what happens in a space is just as important as what stuff is in there. When the organizer delves into clients' habits, preferences, and routines, she starts to see patterns that either help or hurt organization. Some questions to ask about space include:

- What activities are done here?
- Who uses this space? Who should?
- How do these items end up here?
- What doesn't work well here?
- What *does* work well here?

Some questions about personal preference and habits are:

- Are you right- or left-handed?
- Are you a morning person or a night owl?
- Do you learn best through hearing, seeing, or doing?

These questions allow organizers to learn more about the people who use the space and lay the foundation for possible changes.

Danielle had a hard time with clutter in her apartment entryway. Shoes, bags, packages, and mail were always piled there. These would accumulate until she literally tripped as she walked into the apartment. I talked with Danielle and learned that she worked, a lot.

Danielle often came home exhausted at 10:00 or 11:00 p.m. after working fourteen or more hours a day. The mail, bags, packages, and shoes were dropped in the entryway as Danielle made a beeline for bed. Every morning was a scramble as she tried to make it out the door while rummaging through yesterday's things to find her purse, keys, etc. By the end of the week the pile was overwhelming. Some things would be put away, but packages and mail in particular tended to linger for weeks at a time. Understanding Danielle's challenge of working such long hours gave great context to why the entryway was such a hotspot for her. A few organizing products such as a shoe rack and hooks near the door for her coats and bags helped. And we worked out a morning routine that took five minutes to corral the previous evening's mess before she left for work.

Commit to the Change

The third step to overcoming overwhelm is to commit to the change. It is important to set a realistic expectation of the work that needs to be done. Clients need to change habits and behaviors. Without commitment to these changes, organizing efforts are likely to fall short. Organization is the same as any other skill acquired. In the beginning, it is difficult. Clients need to practice, make mistakes, and learn. Commitment to the process of organization is critical to its success. Getting organized is not a straight, clear line. As with therapy, clients occasionally feel times of backslide or regression. At those times clients need to remember their reasons for the change and the steps they've put in place to reach their goals.

Danielle worked hard to not only clear out her entryway, but maintain it as well. This took practice and consistency to create the habit. Occasionally, a tough week or unexpected travel would sideline Danielle's efforts. In the past, she would have thrown up her hands in defeat that her progress stalled. Instead, because she committed to the change and had the necessary tools, she could recall her goal for the space and the steps needed to reclaim it. This empowered Danielle to overcome her overwhelm.

Without commitment, this long-term approach becomes tedious and boring. Commitment doesn't stave off boredom or monotony completely, but at least sets the expectation of the effort and time needed for true change.

Embrace Maintenance

Maintenance is the continual and systematic upkeep of organizing systems that have been put in place. Without maintenance, efforts to organize are siloed into projects. And a freshly organized space quickly becomes a mess again without maintenance. Maintenance is a powerful defense against overwhelm and defeat. Even if the client clears just one surface (the floor, a dresser top, the kitchen table) and sets up a plan for maintenance, it helps provide a clear path for success. Even a small success such as getting all the mail into the designated inbox or doing a five-minute clean up at the end of the day gives a sense of accomplishment, control, and motivation to continue.

With Danielle, once her entryway was in order, she still had other areas of her home she struggled with, such as her closets, kitchen, and dining room. Before we could move on to those, Danielle had to conquer the entryway. The measure of whether or not the entryway was a finished project was if she could maintain its organization. Danielle had to know that she mastered the systems put in place there. Once she was able to consistently maintain the entryway, we moved onto other areas.

In time, a space will need reorganization, even with continued maintenance. Needs for a space change as clients' interests change, family dynamics change, and clients acquire new things. These changes can be gradual and less daunting if a client's space adapts as they happen instead of waiting until they become overwhelming again. The goal isn't to stop life. The aim is to create a space that fits where the client is in life. Since life constantly changes, clients should expect that of their spaces as well.

CHAPTER 16

Lasting Change

M Y OWN HOME HAD a sudden need for reorganization a few years ago. My mother-in-law was having quadruple bypass surgery and my husband and I invited her to recuperate at our home. But with young children and busy schedules, our home and lives were already quite full. Because our home is pretty well organized (I mean, hey, I do this for a living!), rearranging our space wasn't as overwhelming as it could have been. We squeezed my desk and some office supplies into the dining room to create a temporary workspace for me. We borrowed a twin bed and dresser from a family member, and our home office turned into a guest room. To us, this was the epitome of being organized: being able to find what we needed when we needed it. We needed space in our home to welcome Jeanine. And because we are organized, it was easily found.

Whether it is being able to take in a sick family member, find your keys, or simply feel at peace in your home, the intrinsic value of being organizing has its advantages for every family. It removes additional stressors in already busy and chaotic lives. But reaching the state of organized involves so much more than just dealing with the physical stuff.

The nature of organizing work is deeply personal. How can it not be when the organizer is elbow deep in underwear drawers or consoling clients as they sob about a treasured possession? It isn't just about the stuff. It is about so much more.

The mind/home connection is similar to the mind/body connection. These two systems are so intricately woven together. As shown, the home and mind operate the same way.

Separately, organizing work and therapy each create significant benefits for clients. When used together, they support each other to create a holistic environment for change. The underlying principles and practices of therapy and organizing create an environment for clients that is conducive to change. Perhaps those who seek help from professionals are more committed, motivated, or successful in efforts to change. Perhaps there is deeper science at work. Is the connection between the mind and environment more influential than we yet know? Whatever it is, these two worlds come together for the greater good of their shared clients.

> *Professional organizers can be the front line, hands-on support clients need as they tackle emotional decluttering projects, navigate life transitions, and restore order in their homes, lives, and minds.*

I feel privileged that my clients allow me into their homes and their lives to experience this process with them.

Professional organizers can be the front line, hands-on support clients need as they tackle emotional decluttering projects, navigate life transitions, and restore order in their homes, lives, and minds.

Acknowledgements

LUKE, THIS BOOK IS JUST ONE EXAMPLE of how our love and support of each other makes our dreams and goals reality. You are my teammate and partner.

My girls, Ellie and Hana, thank you for putting up with me while I wrote this book. Your patience, support, and encouragement kept me going. I love you both.

To the countless others who helped make this book happen. Among them: my mom and dad, Arlene and Ed Tracy, Matthew Kachersky, Laura Reiss, Deirdre Smith, Kathe Roberts, and Andrea Walker.

To all the professional organizers who bring the craft into clients' homes every day: you help them with so much more than the stuff.

Additional Resources

National Association of Productivity and Organizing Professionals (NAPO)
www.napo.net

Institute for Challenging Disorganization (ICD)
www.challengingdisorganization.org

Clutter Quality of Life Scale
www.challengingdisorganization.org/clutter-quality-of-life-scale--cqls--for-pos

National Association of Senior Move Managers
www.nasmm.org

Association of Personal Photo Organizers
www.appo.org

American Association of Daily Money Managers
www.aadmm.com

Notes

1. Katie Kilroy-Marac, "A Magical Reorientation of the Modern: Professional Organizers and Thingly Care in Contemporary North America," *Cultural Anthropology* 31, no. 3 (2016): 438-457.

2. Kilroy-Marac, "A Magical," 438-457.

3. Kilroy-Marac, "A Magical," 438-457.

4. Ryan Howes, "Why You Lie to Your Therapist," *Psychology Today*, May/June 2019, 44-46.

5. Catherine A Roster, Joseph P. Ferrari, and M. Peter Jurkat. "The dark side of home: Assessing possession 'clutter' on subjective well-being." *Journal of Environmental Psychology* 46, (2016): 32-41.

6. Barbara Hemphill, *Taming the Paper Tiger at Home*, 5th ed. (Washington, DC: Kiplinger Books, 1998), 26.

7. Roster, "The dark," 32-41.

8. Tara Parker-Pope, "A Clutter Too Deep for Mere Bins and Shelves." *New York Times*, Jan 1, 2008, https://www.nytimes.com/2008/01/01/health/01iht-01well.8969298.html.

9. International OCD Foundation, "Diagnosing Hoarding Disorder," Accessed June 30, 2019, https://hoarding.iocdf.org/professionals/diagnosing-hoarding-disorder/.

10. Catherine A. Roster, "Help, I Have Too Much Stuff!: Extreme Possession Attachment and Professional Organizers," *Journal of Consumer Affairs* 49 no. 3 (2015): 303-327.

11. Kilroy-Marac, "A Magical," 438-457.

12. Kilroy-Marac, "A Magical," 438-457.

13. Kilroy-Marac, "A Magical," 438-457.

14. Joseph Ferrari, "Delaying the Decision to Dispose: Research on Procrastination and Clutter Across Age Cohorts, Settings and Object Types," *Institute for Challenging Disorganization* Annual Conference, 2019.

15. Roster, "The dark," 32-41.

16. Catherine A Roster, Joseph P. Ferrari, and M. Peter Jurkat, "The dark side of home: Assessing possession 'clutter' on subjective well-being," *Journal of Environmental Psychology* 46 (2016): 33.

17. Roster, "The dark," 32-41.

18. Roster, "The dark," 32-41.

19. Hormone Health Network, "What is Cortisol," November 2018, https://www.hormone.org/your-health-and-hormones/glands-and-hormones-a-to-z/hormones/cortisol.

20. Jean Chatsky, "One in Four Americans Has a Clutter Problem – And Could be Sitting on Some Serious Cash. *NBC News*, May 31 2017, https://www.nbcnews.com/business/personal-finance/one-four-americans-has-clutter-problem-could-be-sitting-some-n766681.

21. Darby E. Saxbe, and Rena Repetti, "No Place Like Home: Home Tours Correlate with Daily Patterns of Mood and Cortisol." *Personality & Social Psychology Bulletin* 36 no.1 (2010): 71-81.

22. Saxbe, "No Place," 71-81.

23. Saxbe, "No Place," 71-81.

24. Saxbe, "No Place," 71-81.

25. HuffPost, "Home Organization is a Major Source of Stress for Americans, Survey Finds," May 22, 2013, https://www.huffpost.com/entry/home-organization-stress-survey_n_3308575.

26. Susan Krauss Whitbourne, "5 Reasons to Clear the Clutter Out of Your Life," *Psychology Today*, May 13 2017, https://www.psychologytoday.com/us/blog/fulfillment-any-age/201705/5-reasons-clear-the-clutter-out-your-life.

27. Roster, "Help, I," 306.

28. Roster, "Help, I," 303-327.

29. Roster, "Help, I," 303-327.

30. Katerina Karanika and Margaret K. Hogg, "Trajectories Across the Lifespan of Possession-Self Relationships," *Journal of Business Research* 66 (2013): 910-916.

31. Roster, "Help, I," 303-327.

32. Chae (Grace) Boyoun and Rui, Zhu (Juliet), "Environmental Disorder Leads to Self-Regulatory Failure," *Journal of Consumer Research* 40 (2014): 1204.

33. Lissanne Oliver, *Sorted!: The Ultimate Guide to Organizing Your Life – Once and For All*, (New York: MJF Books, 2007), 193.

34. Boyoun, "Environmental Disorder," 1203-1218.

35. Boyoun, "Environmental Disorder," 1203-1218.

36. Boyoun, "Environmental Disorder," 1203-1218.

37. Diane Hatcher, "Are You Affected by Chronic Disorganization?" Fact Sheet 001, *Institute for Challenging Disorganization*, https://www.challengingdisorganization.org/icd-fact-sheets.

38. Mental Health America, "State of Mental Health in America 2018," http://www.mentalhealthamerica.net/issues/state-mental-health-america-2018.

39. Chatsky, "One in Four Americans Has a Clutter Problem."

40. Institute for Challenging Disorganization, "Are you Situationally Disorganized?" Fact Sheet 002, Revised April 2008.

41. Institute for Challenging Disorganization, "Common Characteristics of Chronically Disorganized Individuals," Fact Sheet 003, Revised March 2003.

42. Institute for Challenging Disorganization, Accessed July 1, 2019, https://www.challengingdisorganization.org/.

43. Institute for Challenging Disorganization, "ICD Clutter Quality of Life Scale (CQLS)," 2018, https://www.challengingdisorganization.org/index.php?option=com_content&view=article&id=99:clutter-quality-of-life-scale--cqls--for-pos&catid=20:site-content&Itemid=148.

44. National Association of Productivity and Organizing Professionals, "Our Mission," https://www.napo.net/page/about_napo.

45. Ryan Howes, "Why You Lie to Your Therapist," *Psychology Today*, May/June 2019, 44-46.

46. Joshua F Milburn and Ryan Nicodemus, "Getting Rid of Just-In-Case Items: 20 Dollars, 20 Minutes," *The Minimalists*, https://www.theminimalists.com/jic/.

47. Joseph R Ferrari and Catherine A. Roster, "Delaying Disposing: Examining the Relationship between Procrastination and Clutter Across Generations," *Current Psychology* 37 (2018): 426-431.

48. Ferrari, "Delaying Disposing," 426-431.

49. Ferrari, "Delaying Disposing," 426-431

50. Ferrari, "Delaying Disposing," 426-431.

About the Author

KATIE TRACY IS A CERTIFIED Professional Organizer®, national speaker, and owner of Simple Spaces Professional Home Organizers. Katie appreciates the challenges of jam-packed schedules, overstuffed closets, and simply having too much stuff. Her focus is helping clients find individualized solutions. She truly loves to teach how better organization can help clear not only physical spaces but also bring mental clarity too. Katie enjoys a simple life in New Jersey with her husband and daughters.

.

CPSIA information can be obtained
at www.ICGtesting.com
Printed in the USA
BVHW060523291221
625051BV00012B/1639

9 781734 734089